Outer Banks
Architecture

Outer Banks Architecture

An Anthology of Outposts, Lodges, and Cottages

by MARIMAR McNAUGHTON

John F. Blair, Publisher
Winston-Salem, North Carolina

The paper in this book meets the
guidelines for permanence and
durability of the Committee on
Production Guidelines for
Book Longevity of the
Council on Library Resources.

Library of Congress Cataloging-in-Publication Data
McNaughton, Marimar, 1955–
Outer banks architecture : an anthology of outposts, lodges, and cottages / by Marimar McNaughton.
p.   cm.
Includes bibliographical references and index.
ISBN 0-89587-192-0 (alk. paper)
1. Seaside architecture—North Carolina—Outer Banks. 2. Lighthouses—North Carolina—Outer
Banks. 3. Architecture—North Carolina—Outer Banks. 4. Outer Banks (N.C.)—History. I. Title.
Printed in Canada
NA7575.M37 2000
720'9756'1—dc21   00-023846

Design by Debra Long Hampton

$\mathcal{F}$or
the ones I love,
Mom,
Beau,
and Mere

Contents

Acknowledgments

For opening their doors and their minds, I gratefully acknowledge David Stick; Wynne Dough of the Outer Banks History Center; Richard Darcey, Bob Huggett, and Ken Wenberg of the Chicamacomico Lifesaving Station; Steve Harrison of Cape Hatteras National Seashore; John F. Wilson, A.I.A.; Lloyd Childers of the Currituck Beach Lighthouse; Karl S. Hossli; Edna Baden of the Whalehead Club Preservation Trust; Carl Ross of the Currituck Shooting Club; Roy Sawyer, Jr., of the Currituck County Historical Society; Jeff Davenport of the Pine Island Club; Jack Dudley, author; Peter Rascoe of Preservation North Carolina, Northeast Region; and Doug Brindley, my landlord. For their encouraging words, I humbly thank Angel Khoury, who gave me my first break; Sandy Flickner of *Outer Banks Magazine*; and my dear friends Don and Pat Zerbe, Ellen Wells, Mimi Adams, Jeannine Duke, Miki Jenkins, Ashley Copeland, Ginger Kaufman, Liz Corsa, and Denver Lindley.

Introduction

The Outer Banks oceanfront—150 miles of barrier-island shoreline extending from the Virginia border through Hatteras Island—was virtually unblemished until the early 1800s, when this backdrop of sand dunes and scrub vegetation became the staging area for a series of architectural triumphs that altered the landscape forever.

Such feats as the construction of the second lighthouse at Cape Hatteras were victories of man over nature. The barrier islands are surrounded by shallow water on the west bank and pounding surf on the east bank. They suffer relentless, penetrating northeast winds in fall and winter. In days gone by, there was no urban culture to support such basic human needs as food, clothing, and shelter. And there were very few permanent residents from whom to recruit a labor force. Such were the adversities encountered during the construction of the navigational aids and rescue shelters that were the first fixed structures on the Outer Banks oceanfront.

Despite the odds, the human spirit prevailed,

for establishing lighthouses and lifesaving stations along the coast was of the utmost importance in protecting the country's highly profitable shipping industry and the interests of foreign traders. The lighthouses, light keepers' dwellings, and lifesaving stations that remain are the oldest structures on the Banks. Add to these a few hunt clubs, an enclave of historic summer homes, and the vestiges of the area's first planned ocean-to-sound community and you have this book—an anthology of the outposts, lodges, and cottages that represent the architectural legacy of the Outer Banks.

Light keepers' homes were often constructed from excess materials after a lighthouse was completed. Those built between 1820 and 1870 were simple, single-gabled structures with few embellishments other than porches. By contrast, the light keepers' homes and lifesaving stations constructed in 1874 and 1875—richly textured, excessively decorated outposts that epitomized the fashionable Carpenter Gothic style—were the work of highly skilled architects at the zenith of the shipping industry. By the late 1800s, the Shingle style was in vogue. And when the United States Lifesaving Service commissioned the design and construction of stations in the early 1900s, it introduced yet another architectural style to the barrier islands.

Concurrent with the appearance of light keepers' homes and lifesaving stations near the oceanfront was the construction of privately owned hunting and shooting clubs among the high hummocks bordering the sounds. The few clubhouses that remain range from the Spartan headquarters of the Currituck Shooting Club, the oldest active hunt club in North America, to the lavish Beaux Arts, Art Nouveau, and Art Deco styles of Corolla's Whalehead Club. These exclusive retreats started a trend—one that continues today— in which large gatherings of people of means came to the Banks for a limited season of sport and pleasure.

Vacationing in Old Nags Head took root after the Civil War. To escape the threat of malaria, or "yellow fever," as it was commonly called, privileged families of the upper Albemarle region of eastern North Carolina— planters, doctors, lawyers, merchants, and clergy—established a seaside colony at Old Nags Head, where they hoped to benefit from the prevailing southwesterly winds and light salt air in the spring and summer. The cottages they built to restore the health of farm laborers at the end of the planting season were soon occupied by the wealthy owners themselves. The Old Nags Head cottages comprise an authentic Outer Banks vernacular architectural style. Some of the homes that remain today are owned by members of the original families. The entire community—called "Old Nags Head Beach Cottage Row"—was designated a National Historic District in 1973.

After World War II, when lumber was restricted for government use, visionary artist, civic leader, and real-estate developer Frank Stick launched Southern Shores, a planned ocean-to-sound community, and created the Flat Top, an indigenous architectural style on the northern Outer Banks. The Flat Tops were single-story block cottages made of sand mined from the local beaches, then cast into forty-two-pound cement blocks made in nearby Kitty Hawk village. The first Flat Top, built in 1947, remains today, as do a handful of others from the early period. Many have been razed in recent years in favor of luxury vacation homes, but an interest in retro styles has recently infiltrated popular culture and started an encouraging trend to save and restore the Flat Tops.

The facts, anecdotes, and photos that follow form an anthology of Outer Banks architecture. Only those structures that have been preserved or restored and that remain accessible to the public are covered. The structures range from simple to lavish and represent vernacular as well as formal styles. Using this book as a guide, it is possible for newcomers and old-timers to peel away the excessive commercial and residential development evident on the Outer Banks today and rediscover the barrier islands as they were from the 1800s to the 1950s. It was the structures covered in this book that supported the rustic lifestyle for which the Banks are famous. They also influenced the local building industry and shaped tourism in modern times.

Outposts

Outposts

Light Keepers' Dwellings and Lifesaving Stations

Government-built shelters are the cornerstone of Outer Banks architecture.

Even though permanent settlements had been established along the sound in Currituck County and on Roanoke, Ocracoke, and Portsmouth Islands, lighthouses and homes for their keepers, built from the 1820s to the 1870s, were the first structures erected near the ocean along the barrier islands. These frame-over-timber, masonry-over-timber, or brick homes were straightforward single-family homes or duplex dwellings. Simplicity was the hallmark of these early shelters.

The light keeper's house was modest. It had a kitchen, a parlor, two bedrooms, fireplaces, freshwater cisterns, and an outdoor privy. In the early days, the keeper had only one assistant. Each man pulled a six-hour shift when the beacons were lit between six at night and six in the morning.

The principal keeper and his family shared their home with the assistant keeper and his family. Some houses were made into duplexes, and another house was sometimes added to the light station, especially in the days after the beacons were lit continuously and the light station required three keepers serving eight-hour shifts. Initially, the light keepers' children were home-schooled. They helped with household and lighthouse duties such as cutting the grass, tending the garden, painting the lighthouse, and polishing the lens.

In sharp contrast to the light keepers, the life of surfmen was far from family members and loved ones. Lifesaving station keepers had to be between twenty-four and forty-five years old, able to read, write, and exhibit basic math skills, and demonstrate familiarity of the surrounding waters. They needed extensive experience afloat and had to hire and train their own crews and command men under extremely stressful conditions.

Crewmen had to be at least eighteen years old. They were paid forty dollars a month for a four-month season from December through March. Crewmen were residents of the areas in which they served. Most were experienced fishermen or other types of mariners familiar with local weather, tides, currents, and topographical conditions. Station keepers managed the stations, trained and disciplined the crews, kept a daily log or journal, maintained the weekly schedule, ran the drills, and led the surfmen on all rescue attempts. Each month, the station keeper sent a transcript to the district superintendent.

There were twenty-nine lifesaving station sites on the North Carolina coast that all followed the same regime. On Monday, the surfmen cleaned the station and repaired and polished equipment. On Tuesday, they conducted the surfboat drill. Wednesday was signal flag practice. Thursday was the beach apparatus drill. Friday was first-aid and resuscitation drills. On Saturday, each man did his own laundry. Sunday was for rest and religious expression.

When visibility was good, the watch was from the tower. The lookout kept a record of passing vessels on the sound as well as the ocean. If necessary, signal flags were used to warn mariners of the dangerous shoals. When visibility was poor, crewmen patroled the shoreline between stations, often on foot, sometimes on horseback. A token was exhanged at the halfway mark, a five- to seven-mile round trip. Each man was equipped with a lantern and several Coston lights or flares, used to warn offshore ships.

Unlike the light keepers, surfmen lived away from their families and were given one day a week off to visit relatives.

After 1875, Outer Banks architecture changed dramatically. During Reconstruction, the government employed architects and engineers to design the later lighthouse stations and early lifesaving stations along the Atlantic coast. This new wave of professional architects and engineers who infiltrated the ranks of the Lighthouse Board or worked under the auspices of the Treasury Department for the Lifesaving Service had studied abroad. The government buildings they designed were a blend of classic academic styles imported from Europe and popular regional influences from throughout America in the late 1800s.

During this time, much of the architecture of the late-nineteenth-century keepers' dwellings and surfmen's shelters derived from the Carpenter Gothic style, in which timbered exterior details reflected the infrastructure of the building. The style's exterior patterns utilized horizontal weatherboards with vertical board-and-batten sides. Andrew Jackson Downing, an American landscape architect, ushered the Carpenter Gothic movement into popular culture through the publication of building-pattern books featuring cottages and gardens of the early 1800s. Embellishments such as finials, king posts, crossbeams, buttresses, gargoyles, and arched windows were inspired by the Carpenter Gothic movement of the early nineteenth century and the Renaissance Gothic movement of the late nineteenth century. (Carpenter Gothic and Renaissance Gothic are formal styles frequently combined under the term *Stick style*. However, that term is not used here, so as to avoid potential confusion with the work of Frank Stick, covered later in the book.)

In almost all cases, the lighthouse stations and lifesaving stations were assembled from precut and labeled parts that were hauled by rail, barge, or horse and cart to the site. Despite the strict construction supervision of these federal outposts, the savage weather took its toll on the first 1874 lifesaving stations, which were located precariously near the shoreline to facilitate beach patrols and rescue missions. Many of these stations were destroyed or condemned, and new stations were commissioned on or near the same locations.

The design and construction of these later lifesaving stations was inspired by the progenitor of the American Shingle style, Henry Hobson Richardson. The trend began during the late 1800s and reached its height in the early 1900s. The Shingle style blended contemporary European trends with the aesthetics of colonial America. The rambling floor plans associated with the movement were unified by exteriors clad in cedar shingles and joined under one roof. Two characteristics of the style were sloped gables that extend from the attic to the first floor and exterior walls pushed to the gable ends. The upper rooflines were frequently interrupted by dormers, towers, and turrets. The overall massing of the structures was softened by open porches on the lower floors.

These buildings defined the architecture of the Outer Banks. What started simply became quite complex.

The Outer Banks lighthouse stations have survived, even though some parts have been altered or moved. Only the Currituck Beach Light Station is completely authentic.

By contrast, only three of the twenty-nine Outer Banks lifesaving stations are preserved in their authentic context. The Chicamacomico station in Rodanthe has recently been restored. The Little Kinnakeet station, located near Avon, and the Portsmouth Island station are preserved in states of repose. Other Outer Banks lifesaving stations have been adapted for reuse.

The formal architectural styles they all represent have been recycled again and again. As the past informs the future, so has this architectural legacy shaped the design of contemporary Outer Banks buildings.

Light
Keepers'
Dwellings

Ocracoke Light Station, built in 1823

Ocracoke Light Station
LIGHTHOUSE AND KEEPER'S HOUSE, 1823

The Ocracoke Light Station, established in 1823, was built by Noah Porter of Massachusetts. The original keeper's house was a one-story, single-gabled home completed by Porter in 1824. The three-room home had brick walls sixteen inches thick covered by mortar, then white-washed. The interior walls were plaster painted white.

In 1897, the roof was raised, and a second floor with three rooms was added. The core of this structure is enveloped with additions made in 1928–29 and in 1950.

Cape Hatteras Light Station
LIGHTHOUSE, 1803 AND 1869-70
DOUBLE KEEPERS' HOUSE, 1854
PRINCIPAL KEEPER'S HOUSE, 1871

There has been a lighthouse at Cape Hatteras since 1803, yet the first keepers' house of record, the double keepers' quarters, wasn't built until 1854. It is a frame-over-timber structure set upon masonry piers. Along the south elevation, a one-story porch runs the length of the house. Two single-story kitchens form the wings of the single-gabled structure. The interior rooms are arranged around a side-hall entrance with front and rear access. Two chimneys provide fireplaces for their respective sides of the house, which is divided by a center wall. The double keepers' quarters was renovated in 1892. What was originally the east kitchen was moved to the rear of the structure, and a two-story, sixteen-by-twenty-foot addition was made to the east end.

Though the first beacon at Cape Hatteras was added to, modified, and improved, it still became obsolete. In 1867, the Lighthouse Board ordered a replacement. By 1869, when the second Cape Hatteras Light was nearly complete, the Lighthouse Board assessed the need for a third keeper, which would support an around-the-clock watch. A separate dwelling was built in 1870–71 from surplus bricks and construction materials. Originally intended for use by the third keeper, the house became the residence of the principal lighthouse keeper and his family. The one-and-a-half-story home has a living room, a single-story kitchen, and

Cape Hatteras Light Station,
1854 Keepers' House, 1869 Lighthouse
PHOTOGRAPH BY HENRY BAMBER
COURTESY OF OUTER BANKS HISTORY CENTER

a bedroom on the first floor and two bedrooms upstairs. A single chimney provides fireplaces for the living room and the downstairs bedroom. Additions were later made that expanded the kitchen, the living room, and an upper-level bedroom. Brick foundation walls support the principal keeper's house. As in the case of the double keepers' house, water was collected from the roof and stored in a cistern.

In 1999, the Cape Hatteras Lighthouse and both keepers' houses were moved away from the ocean to a new location twenty-nine hundred feet southwest of the original site.

Principal Keeper's House, built in 1871,
Cape Hatteras Light Station
PHOTOGRAPH BY HENRY BAMBER
COURTESY OF OUTER BANKS HISTORY CENTER

Bodie Island Light Station
LIGHTHOUSE, 1872
DOUBLE KEEPERS' HOUSE, 1872

As soon as construction of the second Cape Hatteras Light Station was completed and the federal government finalized a land transfer for

Bodie Island Light Station, completed in 1872

Cape Lookout Light Station, built in 1872

Photograph by Henry Bamber / Courtesy of Outer Banks History Center

the Bodie Island Light Station, building materials stored at Hatteras were conveyed to Bodie Island. Construction began in June 1871.

The double keepers' house at Bodie Island is nearly identical to the 1854 double keepers' house at Cape Hatteras. The main differences are that the Bodie Island dwelling is built of brick instead of timber over frame and that it has four chimneys instead of two. The side-hall floor plan provides living rooms and kitchens on the lower level and bedrooms upstairs. Front and rear porches run the length of the east and west elevations.

When the Bodie Island Light Station was completed in 1872, a vast quantity of bricks was left over. The engineer recommended using them to build the keeper's quarters at Cape Lookout.

Currituck Beach Light Station
LIGHTHOUSE, 1875
LONG POINT DEPOT HOUSE, 1874
DOUBLE KEEPERS' HOUSE, 1875

As it was in the last century, so it is again today. The heart of historic Corolla is the Currituck Beach Light Station, the last of the first-order lighthouses built on the North Carolina coast.

The four-structure compound—the lighthouse, the double keepers' house, a smaller keeper's house, and a storage shed and privy—is arranged in a quadrangle. The buildings are linked by original brick walkways. The grounds—once a barren, open range but now a dense thicket of loblolly pine, live oak, persimmon, red cedar, and sweet gum trees—are a two-and-a-half-acre oasis within a thirty-one acre parcel that extends from the wetlands of Currituck Sound to the dunes and beaches of the Atlantic. The keepers and their families introduced a new lifestyle to the barren social landscape at Currituck Beach, which was populated by fishermen and farmers—the hunters

Currituck Beach Light Station, completed 1875
PHOTOGRAPH BY HENRY BAMBER
COURTESY OF OUTER BANKS HISTORY CENTER

and gatherers of their day. This was the last unlit portion of the treacherous North Carolina coast.

The government purchased the land for the light station from the Baum and Lindsey families in 1873. From that time until the construction of the lighthouse began in June 1874, the project caused a stir in the neighborhood. Many changes to the local landscape occurred by December 1, 1875, when the lamp was finally lit.

As it was not possible to bring a ship close enough to shore to transport building materials to the lighthouse site, supplies were delivered to Long Point Depot at Churches Island, located twelve miles away across Currituck Sound near the opening of the Albemarle and Chesapeake Canal. That federal transport facility included two Carpenter Gothic dwellings—a two-story duplex and a one-and-a-half-story house—plus storage garages and docks. Construction supplies and equipment were shipped from Hampton Roads to Long Point, where they were stored before being ferried across the sound aboard the *Brooklyn*, a shallow-draft side-wheel steamer. The supplies were unloaded at a dock and delivered to the lighthouse site by rail.

As the light station neared completion, the Lighthouse Board commissioned a double keepers' house, to be built from 1873 plans. The home was completed in 1876. The duplex was embellished with Gothic Revival details in a blending of motifs called Carpenter Gothic, which had been popularized in pattern books prior to the Civil War. The house had two intersecting two-and-a-half-story gables supported by a brick foundation and a full basement. The first level was sheathed in horizontal weatherboards, and the second and attic levels had vertical board-and-batten sides. These vertical planks were shaped into pickets where they joined the horizontal boards. Finials rose from each of the gable ends, which were also punctuated by king posts and crossbeams. The roof was made of cedar shingles.

All of the lumber for the house was precut and labeled. Like the lighthouse parts, it was delivered to Long Point Depot, transported to the construction site, and assembled upon arrival.

The cruciform floor plan was divided into two separate dwellings along the east-west axis. Each residence was a mirror image of the other.

Long Point Depot House, built in 1874, was moved to Currituck Beach Light Station c. 1920

PHOTOGRAPH BY HENRY BAMBER / COURTESY OF OUTER BANKS HISTORY CENTER

Outposts: Light Keepers' Dwellings and Lifesaving Stations 19

The west elevation—where the cross wings project between two one-story shed porches—is intended to be the front. Each shed porch bears chamfered and bracketed posts and a side entrance illuminated by transoms and double-hung windows. A parlor adjoins the center hall at the west entrance. The dog-leg staircases are decorated with turned mahogany newel posts, molded mahogany handrails, and turned balusters. The floors throughout are heart pine. The walls are painted plaster. The foyer and the transverse-hall landing on the second floor have tongue-and-groove pine wainscoting.

Opposite the west entrance are two east-elevation entrances with stoop porches projecting on the cross wing. These entrances are covered by overhanging tent roofs. The irregular center halls connecting the east and west entrances are the primary passageways. Narrow foyers house the stairwells and upper-level landings. The foyers adjoin the kitchens, which are on the east side. The kitchens connect to the dining rooms by way of narrow halls with built-in butlers' pantries. Now that the interior dividing walls have been removed, it is at the intersection of these narrow halls, in the center of the structure, where the cruciform plan is most evident.

On the second floor, where the simple grid is repeated, are three bedrooms for each dwelling and ladder stairs leading to a full attic that provides ample space for storage or an annex for sleeping. The attic's interior is completely clad in horizontal tongue-and-groove pine bead board.

Four elaborate corbel chimneys—one on the north, one on the south, and two in the center—provide fireplaces in all of the ground-floor rooms and the central upper-level bedrooms. Except for the brick-clad hearths in the kitchens, each fireplace has a mantel.

Two keepers and their families shared the dwelling. The light was kept burning for the twelve-hour period from dusk until dawn. Each keeper pulled a six-hour shift—the first from six until midnight and the second from midnight until six.

Square cisterns are located at the northeast and southeast elevations. Both are built over brick-pile foundations, vented with horizontal wooden slats, and covered with board-and-batten hip roofs. The north cistern was doubled in size in 1912, when the first assistant light keeper and the second assistant light keeper and their families shared the north wing of the duplex at a time when the beacon was lit continuously.

It was in 1920 that a smaller keeper's house, built in 1874, was relocated by barge from Long Point Depot to the Currituck Beach Light Station. It was a single-family dwelling also built in the Carpenter Gothic style. The single-gabled, story-and-a-half house had a front porch and a rear shed extension. Like the double keepers' house, it was clad in horizontal weatherboards on the first level and vertical board-and-batten siding on the upper level. The boards were cut into decorative rickrack, and the gable ends were marked by finials and modified king posts and crossbeams. The house was set on brick piers.

An automatic beacon was installed at the lighthouse in 1939, eliminating the need for a manned station. In 1952, the federal government turned the land over to the state of North Carolina, which authorized its Wildlife Resources Commission to conduct muskrat research at the site. In 1973, the first of two applications was filed with the United States Department of the Interior nominating the site for inclusion on the National Register of Historic Places.

In 1979, the site was transferred to the state's Department of Cultural Resources. In 1980, it was leased to Outer Banks Conservationists, a nonprofit organization chartered with the responsibility of restoring the exterior of the house and preserving the site for the public. Outer Banks Conservationists restored the lighthouse (which is now open to the public), the smaller keeper's house (which was then in an advanced stage of disrepair but has since been restored to service as a museum and gift shop), the privy (which is now the organization's office), and the double keepers' house (which is open for special occasions, such as the annual reunion of the light keepers' families). The conservation group manages the facility for the Department of Cultural Resources. The site's annual visitation figure exceeds eighty-three thousand.

The United States
Lifesaving
Service
in North Carolina

The United States Lifesaving Service began in 1848 with a ten-thousand-dollar congressional appropriation to install lifeboat stations along the northeast Atlantic coast. The first of these was built at Spermaceti Cove, New Jersey, in 1849.

However, it was not until 1878, when the Organic Act was passed, that the Lifesaving Service was officially made an agency of the Treasury Department. At that time, coastal outposts were divided into three types. The first, known as "houses of refuge," were shelters for shipwreck victims. They were usually occupied by married couples, who administered first-aid, prepared meals, and sent for help when needed. The second type, lifeboat stations, were equipped for rescues but manned by volunteers. The third type, lifesaving stations, were staffed by professional surfmen and were fully equipped with rescue apparatus.

Hazardous navigation in poorly populated, desolate areas of beach, such as North Carolina's Outer Banks, necessitated the construction of lifesaving stations. In 1874, seven stations were built along the North Carolina coast. The first two, located within what is now Cape Hatteras National Seashore, were the Little Kinnakeet Lifesaving Station, near Avon, and the Chicamacomico Lifesaving Station, in Rodanthe. Others were located at Currituck Beach, Caffey's Inlet, Kitty Hawk, Nags Head, and Oregon Inlet. All seven stations were designed by Francis Ward Chandler, assistant architect of the Treasury Department. In fact, Chandler's designs were used for twenty-three of the twenty-five stations built along the Atlantic coast that year.

New Bern contractor James W. Boyle was hired to build the Little Kinnakeet and Chicamacomico stations at a cost of $2,375 each. However, Boyle's contract to build ten stations in District Six—which stretched from Cape Henry, Virginia, to Cape Hatteras—was terminated after the completion of the Chicamacomico station.

There are detailed accounts of the incendiary interaction between Boyle and government construction superintendents sent into the field to supervise operations. The numerous problems included discrepancies among various sets of building plans, the assembling of construction crews during brutal winter weather, and providing proper shelter and nourishment for the crews. Added to these were the difficulties of shipping building supplies to the Outer Banks and providing proper storage for them.

Lieutenant Stoddard, field inspector for the Treasury Department, ordered Boyle to tear down Little Kinnakeet before the structure was complete, at which point Boyle left the site near Avon and began construction of the Chicamacomico station. Even though he is credited with the construction of the latter station, records indicate that another New Bern carpenter, a D. Simpson, completed the work on Chicamacomico.

Despite such difficulties, a total of twenty-nine lifesaving stations were established along the North Carolina coast between 1874 and 1911. Some have been destroyed by storms and some by fire. Others have been adapted for reuse as rental cottages, restaurants, and retail shops. Only two of the 1874 Gothic-style stations—Chicamacomico and Little Kinnakeet—survive in an authentic setting. And only three of the later Shingle-style stations—the Portsmouth Island station, built in 1894, the second Little Kinnakeet station, built in 1904, and the second Chicamacomico station, built in 1911—have been preserved or restored.

Fortunately, each of the latter three stations represents a distinct architectural type: the Quonochontaug type of the late 1890s (Portsmouth Island), the Southern Pattern of the first decade of the new century (Little Kinnakeet), and the Chicamacomico type of the teens. The most striking difference among these styles is visible in the way the watchtower relates to the primary structure. The Quonochontaug tower blends organically into a gabled roof with sloped sides covered in cedar shingles. The Chicamacomico tower, similar in dimension to the Quonochontaug tower and also located at the gabled end, interrupts the base of the tower where it joins the roofline. The three-story Southern Pattern tower is arranged around a square base and linked to the exterior of the main structure as if it were an addition or an afterthought. Both the Southern Pattern and Chicamacomico-type stations were designed by Victor Mendleheff specifically for the North Carolina coast. Four stations in each style were built on the Outer Banks. None were ever built elsewhere. The two surviving examples are true architectural treasures, especially considering that Mendleheff was the last of the architects for the United States Lifesaving Service.

The Chatham-type stations were

Mendleheff's last design. They closed the chapter on the stations before the Organic Act of 1915 dissolved the Lifesaving Service, which (along with the Cutter Revenue Service) was absorbed by the United States Coast Guard. Seven Chatham stations were built in North Carolina between 1916 and 1927 to replace earlier Outer Banks outposts. Four examples survive: the 1916 Cape Lookout station, the 1918 Creeds Hill station on Hatteras Island, the 1919 Wash Woods station, located near Carova Beach, north of Corolla, and the 1925 Bodie Island station near Coquina Beach, Cape Hatteras National Seashore.

Portsmouth Island Lifesaving Station, 1894 Quonochontaug type,
George Russell Tolman, architect

Portsmouth Island Lifesaving Station
Quonochontaug type, 1894,
George Russell Tolman, architect

The watchtower rises above a ridge of cedar trees on deserted Portsmouth Island. The lifesaving station, equipped, manned, and active in maritime rescue missions a hundred years ago, is now a silent sentry and a totem to the memory of a thriving seacoast town from the 1750s to the 1850s.

Established by the North Carolina assembly in 1753, Portsmouth village was an important gateway to Ocracoke Inlet, which was a major trade route from the Atlantic Ocean to inland ports. Because the inlet's channel was impassable to large sailing ships, Portsmouth village was established to serve as a lightering station. Incoming ships would berth at one of the village's wharves, where goods were unloaded and warehoused, then reloaded on shallow-draft vessels that could navigate Ocracoke Inlet, Pamlico Sound, and the inland waterways. By 1842, two-thirds of North Carolina's exports—mainly tobacco and cotton—passed through Portsmouth, and as many as fourteen hundred vessels sailed through Ocracoke Inlet each year.

In 1860, the population of Portsmouth village peaked at 685. By then, Ocracoke Inlet was shoaling and sea traffic was diverting to Hatteras Island, where a hurricane had opened a new inlet in 1846. Furthermore, the advent of railroads had begun to impact the shipping industry. During the Civil War, many Portsmouth Islanders left the village. Many never returned. Fishing replaced shipping as the primary occupation of villagers. By the time the lifesaving station was built in 1894, the economy of the village was in swift decline.

The Quonochontaug-type lifesaving station that served Ocracoke Inlet is a significant architectural artifact. Located within the historic district of Portsmouth village and listed on the National Register of Historic Places, the station is preserved today by the National Park Service. It is the only Quonochontaug lifesaving station in North Carolina that remains unaltered.

Designed by architect George Russell Tolman for the Treasury Department, the first Quonochontaug station was built at Charlestown, Rhode Island, in 1892. *Quonochontaug* was the Native American name for that area. Such stations often replaced earlier, outdated stations at the same locations.

However, this was not the case at Portsmouth Island, where there was no prior outpost.

The one-and-a-half-story Portsmouth station was covered in cedar shingles. The distinctive hip-roofed watchtower blended into the roofline, with its sloped sides. It was located above the boat room, where double doors on the east and west provided easy access to rescue equipment. The ground-level portion of the station had a wraparound porch and two covered entrances and included the station keeper's quarters and a crew assembly room. The bunk rooms upstairs provided sleeping and storage facilities for seven surfmen. The grounds included a detached cookhouse and a small stable for the horses that were used for beach patrols and for hauling rescue equipment across the sand to the Atlantic Ocean, roughly one mile away.

In many cases, the construction of a lifesaving station in a barren setting spawned the emergence of a surrounding village, since the family members of the surfmen wanted to be near their loved ones. However, Portsmouth village was already well established by the time the need for a lifesaving station was identified. The lifesaving station touched the lives of many Portsmouth Islanders. The crew was recruited from the permanent settlement, and the weekly drills were woven into the fabric of village life.

The all-volunteer crew of the Portsmouth Island Lifesaving Station participated in its first rescue in December 1894. One month later, in January 1895, the keeper received funds to hire surfmen. In 1899, the Portsmouth Island lifesavers rescued six people from two vessels stranded during the San Ciriaco hurricane, which devastated Puerto Rico before unleashing its fury on the southern Outer Banks. But the wreck of the *Vera Cruz VII* was the most dramatic event ever recorded in the station's logbook.

The rescue took place on May 8 and 9, 1903, when the 605-ton brig ran aground in Ocracoke Inlet en route from the Cape Verde Islands to New Bedford, Massachusetts. A total of 399 passengers and 22 crew members were rescued from the stranded vessel during a powerful gale. Of those 421 people, 416 were sheltered and fed in Portsmouth village. Every local man and every boat or skiff available were deployed in the mission. The women of the village prepared over 1,000 meals to feed the survivors and made makeshift beds by laying blankets on the floor in every room of every house. The captain of the vessel fled the scene in an act shrouded in suspicion. He may have been attempting to smuggle Cape Verde Indians into the United States. Or he may have been smuggling cargo—214 barrels of whale oil reportedly worth $6,000. That cargo was also saved by the Portsmouth Islanders.

Little Kinnakeet Lifesaving Station
CHANDLER DESIGN, 1874,
FRANCIS WARD CHANDLER, ARCHITECT
SOUTHERN PATTERN, 1904,
VICTOR MENDLEHEFF, ARCHITECT

The construction of the first of seven identical lifesaving stations in North Carolina began at Little Kinnakeet, near Avon, in 1874. The project tested the relationship between Treasury Department bureaucrats and subcontractors in the field.

What remains of the first, ill-fated structure has been modified twice and moved from its original site. A small addition measuring 5 feet by 19 feet was made to the station in 1885. In 1899, the entire building was condemned after the San Ciriaco hurricane. Repairs were made to the station in subsequent years. Even

though a site for a new station was selected in 1900, no progress was made, and the 1874 station was again condemned in 1902. Finally, in May 1904, the station was moved roughly 1,240 feet away from the ocean.

The Jensen brothers of Racine, Wisconsin, won the rights to build a new station with a bid of $8,800. Construction began in late March 1904. By December 8, the new Little Kinnakeet Lifesaving Station was complete. It was one of only four Southern Pattern stations built in North Carolina.

Victor Mendleheff, architect of the Chicamacomico-type station, has been given credit for the design of the Southern Pattern station as well. The Little Kinnakeet bungalow measured fifty feet along the east-west axis by forty-seven feet wide. It was wrapped by eight-foot verandas on the east and south elevations, connected under one hip roof. The one-and-a-half-story station house was linked to the watchtower, a two-story appendage arranged around a square base and incorporated into the primary structure. Both station house and tower were covered in shingles to unify the exterior. The window trim and the veranda soffits and pilasters were painted white. The tower belting at the first level where it joined the station house was also painted white to re-iterate the tower's connection to the primary structure. Hip-roofed shed dormers interrupted the station-house roof at all four elevations. Clerestory windows surrounded the upper wall of the watchtower.

The primary entrance, on the south elevation, opened into a hall. The station keeper's office was to the right and the crew's day room to the left. In the tower base, left of the day room, was the keeper's private bedroom. The crew's bunk room was on the north side behind the staircase. Along the west side of the first floor were a crew washroom, a closet for foul-weather gear, and a separate washroom for the station keeper. At the northwest corner was utility space for the generator, coal bin, and furnace. Opposite the entry hall was the staircase to the upper level, which was an open space with dormer windows. That space was used for storing equipment and sheltering shipwreck victims. A partition separated this central space from the adjoining tower, where a second night watchman slept while one was on duty. The detached cookhouse and cistern located on the grounds are authentic to the lifesaving station.

Unlike the Quonochontaug- and Chica-macomico-type stations of the early 1900s, the Southern Pattern did not allow for interior boat storage. Rather, the 1874 Little Kinnakeet station was converted into a boathouse. In 1935, the Coast Guard made a ten-and-a-half-foot-wide addition along the east elevation of the 1874 boathouse.

Little Kinnakeet was decommissioned in 1954 and turned over to the National Park Service. Since then, the park service has compiled lengthy reports, conducted paint analysis on the 1874 station, and sketched plans for restoring the entire facility.

Other Southern Pattern stations were built at Ocracoke, Fort Macon, and Bogue Inlet. The Ocracoke station was destroyed in a hurricane in 1946. The Fort Macon station was dismantled in the 1950s. The Bogue Inlet station survived, although it was moved to Cape Carteret, where it serves as a private home. Only the Little Kinnakeet station has been preserved.

The simplicity of the Southern Pattern has been a model to many architects, designers, and builders and a template for the design of new Outer Banks homes and businesses since the early 1980s.

Little Kinnakeet Lifesaving Station, 1904 Southern Pattern; Victor Mendleheff, architect

PHOTOGRAPH BY AYCOCK BROWN / COURTESY OF OUTER BANKS HISTORY CENTER

Chicamacomico Lifesaving Station
1911 Chicamacomico Style (left), Victor Mendleheff, architect;
1874 Renaissance Gothic Style (right), Francis Ward Chandler, architect

Chicamacomico Lifesaving Station
CHANDLER DESIGN, 1874,
FRANCIS WARD CHANDLER, ARCHITECT
CHICAMACOMICO TYPE, 1911,
VICTOR MENDLEHEFF, ARCHITECT

When it was built in 1874, Chicamacomico was the first complete lifesaving station on the North Carolina coast. Even though construction had begun at Little Kinnakeet, Chicamacomico was occupied before Little Kinnakeet was finished. Today, Chicamacomico is the most complete of all such stations on the entire Atlantic coast, in large measure thanks to the preservation and restoration efforts of the Chicamacomico Historical Association. The site includes the original 1874 station, the 1911 replacement station, five outbuildings—two detached cookhouses, a paint shed, a cart house, and a stable—and a cistern as well. The station was active through 1954. The surfmen who served here were highly decorated for their many acts of bravery.

The 1874 Chicamacomico station was designed by Boston architect Francis Ward Chandler, the assistant architect of the Treasury Department. The Chandler-style stations were richly textured, highly decorated structures.

The construction plans and specifications, derived from medieval European influences, had more to do with the education and training of Francis Ward Chandler than the needs of the Lifesaving Service at the time.

Chandler, his contemporary Richard Morris Hunt—architect of George Vanderbilt's Biltmore Estate in Asheville, North Carolina—and his mentor, Alfred Blunt Mullet, are considered by architectural historians to be the spiritual leaders of the Renaissance Gothic style in America. Chandler was among the first students of architecture at Massachusetts Institute of Technology. He and Hunt studied in Paris from 1867 to 1869. When Chandler returned to America, he was an assistant in the Architecture Department at MIT for a brief period. It was then that Mullet, head architect for the Treasury Department, recruited Chandler as his assistant architect, a position Chandler occupied from 1871 to 1874.

Part of his formal education reequired traveling throughout the European countryside sketching buildings of interest to him. Of the 126 drawings he made, 122 were acquired by the DuPont family and are now part of the Joseph Downs Collection of Manuscripts and Printed Ephemera at Winterthur Museum in

Delaware. The Winterthur drawings identify the buildings related to the design of Chandler's 1874 stations. They also show the details that supplied the architect with a vocabulary of Gothic arches and gargoyles, roof angles and eave supports, as well as the post-and-lintel method of construction.

All of these influences came together under the single-gabled roof of the one-and-a-half-story, eighteen-by-forty-two-foot Chicamacomico station. The exterior decoration, which belied the basic purpose of the station, included Gothic arches at the gabled ends and eave supports, dolphin and swan scrollwork, and stylized gargoyles and buttresses. Gothic arched windows and a blind oculus were on the upper level. Board-and-batten vertical siding covered the exterior. Scalloped edges and belting distinguished the upper and lower levels.

The station functioned as a boat-storage shelter and a dwelling for a station keeper and six surfmen. A small living area for the surfman was located on the first floor. The remaining two-thirds of the space was devoted to equipment storage—lifeboat and carriage, life car, Lyle gun, and breeches buoy. Two double doors on the north elevation slid open on rails, and the attached ramp expedited the movement of rescue equipment. Upstairs were a small, private room for the station keeper and a bunk room for the surfmen.

The second Chicamacomico station was built in 1911. It was among the last stations constructed before 1915, when the Lifesaving Service merged with the Revenue Cutter Service to form the Coast Guard.

This larger station, much more residential in appearance than the earlier outpost, improved the quality of life for the surfmen and the keeper. Designs for the station were drafted by Victor Mendleheff in 1910 and adapted from Russell Tolman's Quonochontaug type. Mendleheff's Chicamacomico-type stations were built only in North Carolina, at Chicamacomico and Kitty Hawk.

The Shingle-style exterior features of the one-and-a-half-story Chicamacomico structure included a single-gabled roof with eaves nearly flush with the edge of the exterior wall. The hip-roofed tower erupted from the east gabled end, and hip-roofed dormers emerged from the north and south elevations. The shed-roofed porch on the south elevation was supported by pilasters. The gabled portico at the formal east entrance was supported by pilasters framed with baluster handrails. The tower windows were four-over-four, the upper-level windows six-over-six, and the lower-level windows four-over-two. The entire structure was unified with cedar shingles. All exterior sills, soffits, columns, and railings were painted white. The exterior doors and the porch floors were painted a pale evergreen. The station, the cookhouse, and the cisterns were enclosed by a white picket fence, which was installed to keep out wild pigs and help maintain the lawn.

The original first-floor plan included space for the keeper's quarters, the keeper's office, a day room for the crew, and a boat room. Upstairs were two bedrooms for crewmen and a private room for surfman number one. After 1918, plans were initiated to alter the interior space. By 1925, the boat room was eliminated and its former area designated an assembly room for the crew. The former recreation room became an office for the station keeper, and the original keeper's office became his quarters. His original quarters became a bathroom.

Because of these modifications to the original plan, there were subsequently four entrances. The one on the beachfront elevation opened into a short hall that connected the station keeper's rooms. Two entrances were on the south porch; one of these initially led to the keeper's office, and the other was at the site of the double doors to the boat room. The fourth entrance, on the north side, was close to the cookhouse. It led to a utility space that housed the Delco electric-light plant, the coal furnace, and the laundry room. This area was part of the modifications to the original structure. It was linked to the main building by the bathroom and the storm-clothes closet at the base of the stairwell.

Upstairs were two bunk rooms with closets built into the gabled walls on either side of the dormer windows. Between the bunk rooms was a third room reserved for the inspector.

The enclosed lookout tower on the third level had windows on all four sides and was reached by an interior ladder.

The pine and plaster within the station reiterated the exterior finish. Horizontal tongue-and-groove pine bead board covered the walls in the cloakroom. The window sills, doors, doorframes, floors, and baseboards were also pine. The plaster walls were painted white. Fixtures such as door handles and hooks were made of brass.

The contract for the construction of this station was awarded to Theodore S. Meekins of Manteo for $9,343. When the Chicamacomico

Historical Association restored the structure in 1998, the cost was far greater—$119,000. Since 1974, the historical association has been the shepherd organization for fund-raising, grounds maintenance, and building restoration. It is also, in effect, the curator of the museum and the spark that ignites the living-history interpretations and drill reenactments offered at the site.

Today, the 1911 Chicamacomico station functions as a visitor center. The exhibits on display describe the role of the Lifesaving Service and the Coast Guard in North Carolina.

Chatham-Type Stations
VICTOR MENDLEHEFF, ARCHITECT

In the last years of the United States Lifesaving Service, a new design was introduced to the architecture of the Outer Banks. That design, also believed to have been created by Victor Mendleheff, was called the Chatham type, after the first such station, built in Chatham, Massachusetts, in 1914. The Chatham-type structure was a two-story, five-bay dwelling with a columned portico at the front entrance. The station house was set upon brick piers, and the exterior was clad in weatherboards. The most striking architectural feature was a gable-on-hip-roof combination. The style is easily identified by the absence of an attached, interior watchtower.

The Chatham-type stations on the Outer Banks are Cape Lookout, Creeds Hill, Wash Woods, and Bodie Island. The Cape Lookout station is maintained by the National Park Service. The Creeds Hill station is maintained by Cape Hatteras National Seashore. The Wash Woods station is privately owned by an Outer Banks realty firm and is leased weekly to visitors during the summer months and Bodie Island is owned by Cape Hatteras National Seashore.

Lodges

Lodges

Hunt Clubs
from
Currituck
to
Carteret

A decade before the Civil War, a small group of wealthy Northern sportsmen discovered the hunting grounds along North Carolina's Outer Banks. For several consecutive seasons, their roost was a roadhouse at Van Slyck's Landing, an area now known as Poplar Branch on the Currituck County mainland. By 1857, they had purchased nearly two thousand acres of barrier-island wilderness—marsh islands, wetlands, sand hills, and oceanfront—and established the Currituck Shooting Club, the first of many private hunt clubs on Currituck Sound.

In 1850, the total population of Currituck County—which then included the barrier island from the Virginia line to Cape Hatteras, plus Roanoke Island and parts of the mainland—was 7,227. Of these, 4,600 people were white, 2,447 were slaves, and 180 were free blacks. The social climate was insular. The area's subsistence economy derived almost exclusively from farming, fishing, and hunting.

In the wake of the Civil War, word spread about the wealth of ducks and geese around Currituck Sound, the northernmost pool in the largest estuary in the world. The sound had been a reservoir of brackish water since Currituck Inlet closed in 1828. An underwater garden of eel grass, it was a prime wintering layover for waterfowl along the Great Atlantic Flyway—and thus a prime watering hole for privileged gentlemen from New York, Pennsylvania, and Connecticut.

Northern dollars poured in. Tycoons arrived in this backwater landscape to reap the spoils of war and take refuge within what some called the "Cornucopia of Life." The Currituck, as advertised, was a "Sportsman's Paradise." Northerners bought up land that had been granted to local families since the Revolutionary War, established hunting rights, and set up lodges. Their arrival was considered a harbinger of good times, as the newcomers would create an entire season of game hunting every fall and winter. Their dependence upon the locals during their stay meant that everyone would profit from their coming. The exclusive clubs they built, owned by members-only syndicates, seeded the tourism industry that would later flourish along the Outer Banks.

Currituck's clubs were, in north-south order, the Currituck Sound Club, the Swan Island Club, the Monkey Island Club, the Narrows Island Club, the Lighthouse Club, the Currituck

Shooting Club, and the Palmer Island Club. Of this lot, the Currituck Sound Club has been relocated to Knotts Island, where it is open to the public; the Swan Island Club is owned by the Nature Conservancy; the Monkey Island Club is owned by the United States Fish and Wildlife Service; Narrows Island was purchased by the Currituck Shooting Club in 1933, was sold again in 1946, and was bought by Earl Slick of Winston-Salem in 1967; the Lighthouse Club, sold in 1919 and again in 1922, is now the site of the Whalehead Club in Corolla; the Palmer Island Club, disbanded in 1906 and subsequently renamed Pine Island, is also owned by Earl Slick. Only the Currituck Shooting Club, listed on the National Register of Historic Places, remains authentic to its origins. It is the oldest active hunt club in continuous operation in North America.

The Currituck hunt clubs flourished into the early 1900s. Meanwhile, other North Carolina hunting grounds were discovered at Lake Mattamuskeet, Core Sound, and Oregon Inlet. Nonetheless, Currituck Sound retained its position as the greatest waterfowl-hunting area in the state.

The hunting industry peaked during the years leading up to World War I but came to a halt in 1916, when the United States and Great Britain signed a treaty prohibiting the sale of wild waterfowl in the United States and Canada. Designed to protect migratory birds by prohibiting market hunting, the treaty posed a threat to the economy of Currituck County. Despite the setback, the hunt clubs continued to thrive. The wealthy elite kept coming to Currituck Sound until the Great Depression. Many clubs folded in 1930. In an ironic twist of fate, droughts struck the Canadian breeding grounds and decimated the migratory waterfowl population around that same time. In the years since, efforts to restore the breeding grounds were initiated by two Currituck Sound sportsmen, Joseph P. Knapp and Thurmond Chatham. Through their efforts, a private organization, Ducks Unlimited, was formed to restore the Canadian watering holes and resurrect the dying waterfowl population.

Hunt clubs appeared in the Core Sound area in the last quarter of the nineteenth century and the first quarter of the twentieth century. Due to the fragile nature of the southern Outer Banks and the remoteness of the hunting grounds from major metropolitan areas, the Core Sound clubs did not survive the ravages of storms and economics. The Core Sound clubs were, in north-south order, the Harbor Island Club, the Hog Island Hunting Club, the Pilentary Hunting Club, the Carteret Gun and Rod Club, and the Davis Island Hunting Club.

Currituck Shooting Club, 1879
The oldest active hunt club in North America dates its membership to 1857.

PHOTOGRAPH BY RAY MATTHEWS

Birds of a Feather

The Currituck Shooting Club
1879

The brick-red plumage of the Currituck Shooting Club's chimneys comes into view from the fifth tee of the Currituck Club Golf Course. Electric carts whiz past the exclusive roost of an endangered species—the last eleven members of the oldest hunt club in North America.

The cedar-shingled barn of a building erupts from the meticulously maintained golfscape. It is three stories high, four bays wide, and seven bays long. Even though the club dates to 1857, the clubhouse used today was built in 1879. The imposing single-gabled structure, the club's second headquarters, is listed on the National Register of Historic Places.

Much of the lumber for the clubhouse was precut and sent down on barges from New York. Most of the wood was heart pine and cypress, to resist termites. Like many of the government-built structures of the era, the house was assembled on the site. Framed in the balloon method—without posts and crossbeams—it had only one ground-level sill, and the vertical beams extended all the way to the top floors.

The architect is not known, though it is speculated that H. H. Richardson, the father of the American Shingle style, might have had a hand in designing the clubhouse. Some feel it is unlikely that Richardson would have designed such a Spartan dwelling. Others suggest that Richardson's protégé, Stanford White, an occasional guest at the Currituck Shooting Club, was the architect and that the style is markedly similar to White's Shinnecock Hills Country Club on Long Island, New York. This rumor is unsubstantiated.

Its shingled exterior notwithstanding, the Currituck Shooting Club had little to do with the Shingle style, in which a rambling floor plan was unified under one roof and blended with exterior shingles for an overall homogenized look. In fact, the Currituck Shooting Club had ground-floor common areas and upper-level dormitory-style sleeping rooms not unlike the private, all-male academies that flourished in the Northeast in its day.

The Currituck Shooting Club's membership roster could have been lifted from the society pages of the *New York Times*. Some of the country's leading industrialists and philanthropists were the founding members of this elite group. Valentine Hicks visited Currituck in 1854 and discovered the bounty of ducks and geese there. On April 14, 1857, Hicks and Stephen Tabor purchased approximately seventeen hundred acres from Abraham Baum for three thousand dollars. On June 8 of that year,

fifteen charter members met in the offices of Philo T. Ruggles, Esq. They formed an association governed by a constitution and bylaws and established twenty-one shares in the Currituck Shooting Club.

Except for the Civil War years, the club has operated continuously since then. Until 1947, the members were exclusively Northerners. They traveled by rail to Cape Charles, Virginia, ferried across Chesapeake Bay to Norfolk, and engaged a horse and carriage (or, later, an automobile) to take them to Munden's Point, Virginia. From there, they sailed down Currituck Sound to Van Slyck's Landing and then across the sound—most likely aboard the *Cygnet*, the shooting club's classic yacht in the early 1900s. Each member received a deed, a key to his room, a skiff for transportation from the club to the blinds, a set of decoys, and the privilege of walking freely into the club room.

Despite the geographic and social distance from centers of business and culture and the purposely cultivated rustic lifestyle at the club, the members enjoyed certain amenities during their sojourns. One of these was provided by May Halyburton, wife of the *Cygnet*'s engineer, Harry Halyburton. Mrs. Halyburton was responsible for obtaining stock reports. She would telephone the keeper of the weather station at Cape Henry, Virginia, with instructions, after which the keeper, a Mr. Newsome, would place a call to Wall Street. Newsome would then phone Mrs. Halyburton with the numbers, which she wrote down and gave to the butler, who delivered them on a silver tray into the club room.

Among the esteemed members were J. P. Morgan, W. K. Vanderbilt, and Henry O. Havemeyer, president of the American Sugar Refining Company (later Domino Sugar). A group of members led by William P. Clyde endowed Poplar Branch High School in 1907. Other members wrote treatises extolling the virtues of the Currituck region. In 1925, Samuel Russell published *History and Notes Relating to the Currituck Shooting Club*. An article entitled "Currituck Sound" by Frederick C. Havemeyer II appeared as a chapter in *Duck Shooting along the Atlantic Tidewater*, released in 1947 by William Morrow and Company.

During the club's lengthy history, it has had only six superintendents. Of these, John W. Poyner served the longest, from 1909 to 1960. His tenure began at the height of waterfowl hunting and survived two world wars, the end of market hunting in 1916, the Great Depres-

sion, and the decimation of the migratory waterfowl population due to droughts in the Canadian breeding grounds in 1930 and 1931. His daughter, Mary Poyner Glines, born in 1906, lived at the club from the time she was three. Her mementos and vintage photographs are exhibited at the Currituck County Library in Barco. Through her recollections, county historians are compiling the legacy of the Currituck Shooting Club.

The geese and ducks still return to Currituck Sound every fall and winter. Today's club members arrive like clockwork in November and lay over through December and late into January. Even though the club can be reached by modern roads, Carl Ross, a Currituck native and the club's superintendent since 1977, prefers traveling as members did back in the old days, departing by boat from the mainland, crossing the sound, and covering the west lawn of the Currituck Shooting Club on foot.

The gray door swings into a white hallway, where a dozen identical pine doors line up shotgun style down either side of the corridor. Each door is marked by a hand-painted porcelain tile or an engraved brass plate.

Located to the left behind doors number

1 and 2, the club room overlooks the west lawn and the sound beyond. The Arts and Crafts–style Morris chairs are arranged in a half-circle around the hearth. A molting American eagle hangs from the ceiling above the fireplace. Glassed cabinets contain an example of every kind of duck-billed bird known to the shooting club's members. A snow goose hangs in the southwest corner. The rooftop weather vane is connected to a compass in the ceiling of this great room, allowing the members the luxury of knowing the wind direction without ever having to leave the cozy den. In this room of trophies, the real prize is the game register—three leather-bound volumes of shooting records dating from 1888 to 1987, filled with handwritten entries that chronicle kills like the one at Old North Pond, where 5,004 birds were bagged in 1918. The quota, once 25 ducks and 10 geese per man per day, dwindled to 3 of each per man per day. On January 17, 1987, this last entry was written: "The end. A poor end to a poor season. Only half the ducks seen as last year." No formal shooting records have been kept since 1987.

The club room is flanked by the bar, where rows of locked cupboards bear the names of members. Beyond the bar are the dining room, which also overlooks Currituck Sound, and a spacious double kitchen. To the right of the main entrance, what was originally a bedroom has been converted into an ammunition room, where members store and clean their guns. Between the ammunition room and the stairs at the end of the hall are a bathroom and four bedrooms.

On the second floor, also arranged along a central hall, are the members' quarters, simply furnished with single beds and bureaus. White bead-board wainscoting covers the lower walls (where the original horsehair plaster got loose), but the upper walls vary greatly. Shades of vermilion, forest green, moss, and even Wedgwood blue distinguish one old bird's coop from another, each nest feathered with duck stamps, decoys, and personal esoterica. In honor of the first Southern member, Congressman Thurmond Chatham, who was admitted to the club in 1947, the upstairs latrine is named Chatham Hall. The room of extinct member Cornelius Mitchell has been set aside as a living-history museum. It features fossils from the 1880s to the 1920s, such as an original potbelly stove, a washtub and basin, and a

Delco electric power bar beside an iron-frame bed.

On the third floor, now sealed off, are four large bedrooms that were used by the gentlemen's men and their private cooks.

In the Currituck Shooting Club's heyday, its twenty-one members and their guests were aroused by the rising sun. After hurriedly eating breakfast, they scrambled for guns, ammunition, and decoys in a mad dash for the boat landing. From there, they raced in skiffs to the coveted southeast point, known as Indian Gap. These days, the eleven members who ante up big bucks in initiation fees for a forty-five-day season find it more important to have a good housekeeper and good cooks than good guides. Their afternoon and evening meals begin with popcorn, peanuts, and wine, followed by oysters on the half shell, smoked salmon on crackers, and steamed shrimp, followed by roast duck or grilled lamb. They enjoy Heineken on tap, port, and cigars.

What started in 1857 with roughly 1,700 acres eventually grew to 6,000 acres. In 1977, the syndicate sold three miles of oceanfront for $1.3 million. The tract included the Poyner's Hill sand dune, which was leveled for the de-velopment of Ocean Sands. That left 2,000 acres of marsh and 600 acres of highlands, on which the members paid $3,300 in property taxes. Five years later, that tax increased to $5,500. It continued climbing until it leveled off at $25,000. Then it jumped again, skyrocketing to $157,000 by 1989.

In late 1989 and early 1990, the members considered cashing in. They reached a tentative agreement with Boddie-Noell Enterprises of Rocky Mount, North Carolina, yet negotiations continued until 1993, when the corporation broke ground on the Currituck Club, an eighteen-hole golf course and residential community. The Currituck Shooting Club's deal left the members owning half interest in the lots sold for residential development, but their own private property was reduced to thirteen acres of high ground. They retained hunting rights. Luxury home sites and a Rees Jones golf course have been carved out of the barrier-island wilderness, yet the Currituck Shooting Club is behind an anchor-black, chain-link fence.

These days, most birdies are shot from tee to green.

Whalehead Club, completed in 1925, was erected near the site of the old Lighthouse Club.
It was originally christened Corolla Island by Edward Collings Knight, Jr.
PHOTOGRAPH BY RAY MATTHEWS

Once upon Corolla Island

The Whalehead Club
1925

A watery ring surrounds the Whalehead Club. A moat marks the entrance to this, the crown jewel of historic Corolla village. Tales about the mansion, formerly known as Corolla Island, and its eccentric occupants are still told by local people. In doing so, they uphold a richly textured oral tradition inspired by the life and times of Edward Collings Knight, Jr., and his second wife, the former Marie Louise Lebel.

As the story goes, it was 1920 when Knight first visited the Outer Banks from Philadelphia. Born in 1863, he would have been in his late fifties. His first marriage, to Clara Dwight, ended when she passed away. The couple had one daughter, also named Clara. Their summer place was the opulent Claraden Court in Newport, Rhode Island.

The heir to a fortune earned by his father, an inventor and entrepreneur, Knight presumably came to Currituck to hunt. He was a guest of the Lighthouse Club. In 1922, he purchased the club from the Davis brothers, who had bought the property from the original owners three years earlier. Knight alledgedly wanted to create a new club for his second wife, a French Canadian and a huntress who had been denied entry to the all-male hunt clubs of Currituck Sound.

Knight wasted no time preparing the site for his lodge. He dredged up the land along Currituck Sound near Lighthouse Cove to create a man-made island. On it, he built a house that eclipsed all others on the Outer Banks in size, scale, grandeur, and amenities. Corolla Island took three years to build, as construction proceeded only during the Knights' sojourns in the fall and winter months. When the Knights' house was inhabitable, the old Lighthouse Club was dismantled. The structure, though not grand by Knight's standards, was lavish for the Outer Banks. Some say the extravagant architecture was intended to vindicate the shunned Mrs. Knight.

When finished in 1925, Corolla Island was the only three-story house on the Banks. It had a reinforced-steel I-beam frame, a sixteen-room basement, an electric generator, a coal-fired furnace, steam radiators, an Otis elevator, a dumbwaiter, fresh and salt running water, brass pipes, and lead drains. The covered boathouse and swimming pool came later. All in all, Corolla Island was a lavish retreat—a French country chateau in Currituck. The structure measured approximately twenty-three thousand square feet, nineteen thousand of which were usable space. It supposedly cost $383,000 to build,

although it has yet to be determined how much Knight paid for the Lighthouse Club and its grounds. The design incorporated the best attributes of three significant early-twentieth-century styles—Beaux Arts, Art Nouveau, and Arts and Crafts.

The core of the house—five bays wide—was flanked on either side by wings, each two bays wide. The first-floor exterior was distinguished by sets of windows and the second-floor exterior by dormers. Each wing had an open balcony on the second floor, where a decorative water lily relief was carved into belting between the first and second floors. The house was originally painted a brilliant shade of yellow trimmed in terra cotta.

Five chimneys erupted from the copper-shingled roof. Four of these were true chimneys. The fifth—the central chimney—was false. Its interior structure, housed in the fourth-floor attic, contributed to the home's ventilation system. The rafters extended from the attic roof to the first floor. As warm air collected at the lower levels, it rose by way of the open rafters into the attic. The false chimney had windows on either side that allowed the warm air to pass through the opening in the roof. But what is perhaps a better explanation for the fifth chimney derives from an oral legend passed down by villagers when the house was under construction. It seems that Mrs. Knight, in her effort to one-up her wealthy hunt-club neighbors, was determined to have one more chimney than the Currituck Shooting Club, which had four.

Wild horses once grazed on the south lawn. Cattails, water lilies, and morning glory grow in abundance on Corolla Island. Indeed, it was the flora, not the ubiquitous waterfowl, that inspired the decorative motifs and interior details wrought in brass, glass, and mahogany. Some of these interior details—like the carved florets, moldings, and light fixtures—appear to predate the construction of the house. Their origins, along with the identity of the architect, designers, and artisans, have not yet been determined.

The primary entrance, on the south porch, offered a stunning view of Currituck Sound. The grand hall intersected the foyer at this entrance. There was a duplicate doorway on the north wall. The sidelights allowed a glimpse of the harbor, the 1926 boathouse, the Chippendale footbridge, and the neighboring Currituck Beach Lighthouse.

To the west of the grand hall was the library, which doubled as a ballroom. Five entrances led to and from this space—one from the grand hall, one from the service pantry, one from the south porch, and two from the west porch. All were wrapped in molded mahogany pilasters. Morning glory vines were hand-carved into the mahogany hearth, their shoots budding into the pilasters on either side. The built-in window seats on the north and south sides of the room were flanked by built-in bookshelves. Behind each of the four bookshelves were steam radiators. The steel support beams running the length of the ballroom ceiling were clad in mahogany panels, as were the walls throughout the room. For the ballroom, the Knights purchased a low-signature 1902 Steinway sketch piano (a one-of-a-kind instrument made from custom drawings).

The water lily prevailed in the dining room, located at the east end of the grand hall. Stems grew out from between the wall panels and erupted near the ceiling into hand-carved blossoms in relief. The wallboards were pale pearl gray with dove gray accents. The Tiffany brass chandelier bore the image of cattails. The sixteen Tiffany wall sconces—eight in the dining room and eight in the grand hall—had brass bases with white-and-green globes also inspired by the water lily. The water lily motif continued in the custom furniture; it was hand-carved into the legs of the dining-room table and across the facade of the breakfront sideboard. These and the Steinway are the only authentic furnishings and fixtures in the house today. It is believed that the missing silver flatware also bore the water lily theme.

The floors throughout the house were clad in cork tiles, which were hand-waxed and buffed to a high gloss. The walls of the second-floor bedrooms (including the servants' quarters), the ground-level foyer, and the upstairs halls were tongue-and-groove pine corduroy routered into one-inch wales. The Art Nouveau staircase was encased in hand-carved mahogany.

Beneath the stairs on the first floor was the electrical panel, on which enamel labels designated each room of the house—the Lilac Room, the Blue Room, the Pink Room, and so on. A buzzer board in the kitchen was similarly marked. On the north side of the first floor were an office, a gun room, a mud room, and a dining room for the domestic staff, along with a back stairway from the kitchen to the servants' quarters on the second and third floors.

The second floor contained two private suites—one on the southwest corner for Mrs. Knight, the other on the northwest corner for Mr. Knight. Both rooms offered views of Currituck Sound through glass doors that led to an open balcony on the west elevation. Each room had a fireplace. Mrs. Knight's mantel and surround were carved wood in a leafy anthemion pattern, while Mr. Knight's surround was hand-painted clay tile. There were false doors that appeared to connect the two rooms; the door on Mr. Knight's side did not open. Mrs. Knight's suite was equipped with three half-closets built into the dormered alcove walls, while Mr. Knight's had three half-closets in the bedroom, plus a dressing alcove and triple-closet arrangement located between his bedroom and bathroom. The triple closet was comprised of a walk-in closet with rods, which opened into an inner closet with shelves, which bore the door to a secret storage area. Mr. Knight's double bathroom—two sinks, two water closets, two tubs—was shared with an adjoining guest room. That room was often occupied by Charles Browne, a family friend and perennial houseguest. All the bathrooms in the Knights' suites and the guest rooms were decorated with yellow ceramic tiles and Tiffany crystal towel bars. Both fresh and salt water were piped into the custom-sized claw-foot porcelain tubs in the Knights' suites. Mrs. Knight's bathroom was equipped with a bidet. There were three more spacious guest suites on the second floor, all with private bathrooms and connecting pocket doors.

An elevator served the entire house from basement to attic. Trunks were delivered to the basement. After they were unpacked, their contents were hauled to the second floor aboard the vintage counterweight lift.

Two linen closets were located in the guest hall, which connected to the maids' quarters through a maze of narrow passages. Of the four rooms occupied by servants, three shared a common bathroom and one was a private suite. Two of these rooms enjoyed the use of the open balcony on the east elevation.

The spacious servants' quarters on the third floor consisted of one large room that extended the entire length of the house.

It is not known which servants' rooms were occupied by males and which by females.

The Knights planted live oak trees on the grounds and built two Chippendale bridges for foot traffic across the moat. One of those bridges remains and has been restored.

The boathouse, built in 1926, served as a boat-storage facility and also housed a grain elevator, a warehouse, and an office. Among the structure's many unique qualities were the symmetry of the arched openings and covered porches, the pitch of the hip roof and the eaves, and the blue-painted back wall that appeared to vanish when approached from the water. There were two covered slips in the center of the boathouse. On the west side was a system of pulleys designed to hoist craft into the air for dry storage. On the east side was the grain elevator, designed to dispense the grain stored on the second level, which was used for feeding geese and ducks. On the back of the east wall were metal pipes arranged vertically, to which ducks were tied to cure. This area was ventilated by a louvered wooden facade. In the rear of the boathouse was a raised platform with steps on either side. It is said that Mrs. Knight welcomed boats in from the hunt from this staging area, and that the elaborate footbridges were designed for her use in traveling to and from the lodge.

Despite the first-rate accommodations and the extensive grounds, it seems that no more than three guests at a time—and only twenty-five guests altogether—visited the Knights in the eleven years that they occupied the house.

The home's logbook, which once belonged to the Lighthouse Club, was meticulously maintained by Mr. Knight and embellished with his holiday drawings of trimmed Christmas trees and Thanksgiving turkeys. It is said that the Knights were generous to the local people, although Mrs. Knight earned a reputation for mannish dress and roguish manners.

When Knight died in 1936, Mrs. Knight inherited Corolla Island. At her death several months later, the house became part of their estate. Knight's only daughter had preceded him in death, so his two granddaughters were the only heirs. Both young women were married and living in Europe and had no use for a hunting lodge in Currituck County, North Carolina.

In the ensuing years, the home was sold several times before a failed development plan led to bankruptcy. Currituck County bought the house and twenty-eight acres of land at auction for $2.4 million in 1992. The county acquired an additional ten acres in 1994, the same year it appointed the Whalehead Club Preservation Trust to restore the facility and create an on-site museum showcasing Currituck's waterfowl heritage. Today, this non-profit, volunteer board of directors works closely with members of the Currituck Wildlife Guild. It is hoped that the two organizations and Currituck County will come to an agreement about how the grounds should be developed for use as a wildlife interpretive center and a public gathering area for outdoor concerts and festivals.

Regardless of the site plan's final outcome, the Whalehead Club will be the centerpiece. It is anticipated that the restoration will be completed by 2003, at a cost of $5.5 million. In the process, the restoration architect and his team will re-create a complete set of plans, as the originals have never been found. These drawings are expected to include 120 pages of floor plans, plus mechanical, electrical, fenestration, finish, detail, and hardware schedules.

Many questions have been answered during the restoration, but just as many new ones have been raised. Chances are these mysteries will not solve themselves. If so, the legends passed from villagers and tour guides to visitors will continue to immortalize the eccentric occupants of Corolla Island in a fairy tale without an ending.

Pine Island Audubon Sanctuary

The Pine Island Club
1913

On the first Sunday in December each year, the grounds of the Pine Island Club are open to members of the National Audubon Society for the annual Christmas bird feeding.

Barely visible to the untrained eye, screened by a natural cover of pine and bayberry, the entrance to Pine Island is two miles north of Sanderling. Over one hundred geese—mostly Canadian, two calico, and a lone white goose—wander freely across the front lawn. The club's caretakers raised these wildfowl from hatchlings in two-by-two-foot boxes filled with straw. After their evening feed, the geese waddle into a large waterfront pen beside Currituck Sound.

This hunt club was organized in 1850 under the name Palmer Island Club. One published account of the club's history says that Josephus Baum, an Outer Banks farmer, owned the club and the surrounding grounds and

The current Pine Island Club was the second clubhouse built on the site of Palmer Island Club.

leased them to private groups. Another version suggests that Baum purchased the club when it disbanded in 1906 and then leased the marsh islands and the clubhouse to private groups. Both accounts concur that the property was sold for $60,000 in 1910 to a group of Boston businessmen led by Preston Clark. The new members renamed the club Pine Island. In 1935, the Boston group sold the Pine Island Club to Austin Barney of Farmington, Connecticut, for $25,000. In 1972, Barney's heirs sold the lodge and the land to Earl Slick of Winston-Salem for $2.7 million. Slick subsequently deeded fifty-three hundred acres of his northern Outer Banks property to the National Audubon Society, as the ocean frontage and wetlands were a prime wintering spot for shorebirds and waterfowl along the Great Atlantic Flyway. Through his gift, Slick established the Pine Island Audubon Sanctuary and preserved the last undeveloped barrier-island wetlands on Currituck Sound for migrating geese and ducks.

Among the most dramatic events that occurred on these grounds was the fire that leveled the original clubhouse in 1913. The clubhouse was rebuilt within six months of the disaster. Little else has caused a stir, perhaps due to the private interests of Austin Barney and Earl Slick, whose ownership covered two-thirds of the club's history. Both used the club as an exclusive retreat for themselves, their families, and their close friends. Indeed, change has been slow in coming to Pine Island, even though neighboring Currituck hunt clubs have weathered drastic transitions in recent years, either through the sale of property or the liquidation of assets.

The lodge is a very simple two-story wood-frame house massed in three two-story bays connected under one hip roof. Two single-story additions join the central structure on the north and south elevations. The primary entrance—the single embellishment in an otherwise straightforward structure—is announced by a lipped shed roof supported by four pilasters. To ease maintenance, the lodge's exterior has been wrapped in gray siding. The window frames, soffits, and pilasters are painted white.

Inside the foyer is the central stairwell with its walnut-stained newel posts, balustrades, and handrails. Its oyster-white plaster walls are draped with jewel-toned handmade quilts. The living room, located on the right, is original to the structure, but the adjoining Florida room was added in 1980. In the dining room, directly opposite the main entrance, the pine floor is clear-finished, and the pine doors, frames, window sills, and wainscoting are stained a dark walnut; again, the plaster walls are oyster white. A remarkable collection of Blue Willow Ware serving plates and dishes salvaged from the clubhouse fire are grouped for display, decorating the otherwise bare walls of the living and dining rooms. In this spartan setting, there is but one nod to excess. Recessed in a corner of the dining room is a pine-paneled niche. A dozen liquor cabinets line the interior wall. Clear-glass wood-framed doors reveal the contents of this once-secret stash. This alcove is paneled in tongue-and-groove bead board stained a dark walnut.

The five-bedroom lodge and two cottages—one for the club's manager and the other for its caretakers and hunting guides—are the primary structures at the Pine Island Club. In addition to the goose pen, there are chicken and dog pens, a garage, four guest cottages, and a private airstrip.

The boat landing is the real staging area

for the club's activities. The manager and three caretakers maintain the boat docks and the two outbuildings, which shelter hunting boats and decoys dating back to the club's beginnings. During the mellow days of Indian summer, this team gathers at the landing and waits for the tide to rise before setting out to cut fresh corn sedge and prepare the blinds for duck-hunting season, which begins in early November.

The team travels in flat-bottomed sedge boats locally made from juniper. One boat, fitted with an outboard motor and equipped with two poles, two chain saws, and a gas can, tows the other. The second boat is also equipped with poles and carries a handful of one-by-three-inch boards. Years ago, both boats would have been poled to a nearby marsh island, where the occupants would have cut the abundant sedge with swing blades instead of chain saws. But these are the only differences in a tradition established nearly one hundred years ago.

Within an hour, the four-man team whacks a boatload of sedge. In a good year, this is enough for seven or eight blinds, but other years, the sedge has taken a beating from late-summer storms and is somewhat trashy. Three men pass about thirty bundles of sedge to the fourth man, who arranges the reedy stalks in the back of the boats and secures the loads with the one-by-three-inch boards. In fifteen minutes, the sedge boats are loaded. In another fifteen minutes, the caravan arrives at one of the fifty-eight blinds that need refurbishing each season. "Sticking" a blind takes thirty to forty-five minutes. The men wedge fistfuls of sedge in the frame of the two-man blind. The chain saws provide the finishing touch, trimming the grass to shoulder height in front and just over head height in back.

Working at this rate, the team makes five or six blinds a day for the better part of two weeks—providing the weather is good. From November until late January, these same four men lead every hunting party that visits Pine Island.

From the marsh, the shiny, silver roof of the Pine Island Indoor Racquet Club eclipses the view of the old clubhouse chimneys. Along the horizon, cookie-cutter houses line the oceanfront like hotels on a Monopoly game board. Two water towers—one in Duck, the other at Ocean Sands—and two telecommunications towers further interrupt the serene setting. This time of year, flocks of black cormorants signal the onset of autumn. Commercial airliners leave white streaks across the Great Atlantic Flyway.

Despite the intrusions, Pine Island is a paradise preserved, an oasis in a sea of change.

Cottages

Cottages

Old Nags Head
and
Southern
Shores

Old Nags Head:
Beach Cottage Row

A colony of prosperous planters arose in eastern North Carolina over one hundred years ago. They left the fertile delta—the sea floor in ancient times—and traveled downriver from their Albemarle plantations by steamer toward the Atlantic for the summer cure. It was believed that the fresh air and salt water were tonic for the "yellow chills," or "yellow fever," as malaria was commonly called.

Only families with the wherewithal to pack up the entire household and enough provisions to last for months could afford to spend the season. These families came from the upper regions of the Albemarle—Edenton, Hertford, Windsor, and Elizabeth City. Initially, they brought their slaves to the shore to rest and restore their health after a season of planting. But in the wake of the Civil War, it was the planters' wives and children, neighbors and friends, cooks and maids, chickens and cows that occupied the rustic cottages and the surrounding property. The

A sound-side view of Old Nags Head showing the post office (left) and bathhouse (center)

families of doctors, lawyers, and merchants came next. The waterfront colony they sowed on Roanoke Sound became the first Old Nags Head—a crop of cottages, a general store, a post office, and a bathhouse. Nothing of that colony survives on its original site today, though some people believe that one or two cottages were moved to the second Old Nags Head, on the oceanfront, where they have been added to over the years.

Out of the need to restore health emerged a tradition of summering that has lasted many generations. As early as 1866, houses began to appear on the oceanfront. Thirteen original homes seeded the famous Old Nags Head colony. These and more than sixty others built before the late 1930s comprise Old Nags Head Beach Cottage Row, a National Historic District. Established in 1977, the district covers one mile of barrier-island oceanfront. The Old Nags Head style derives from this enclave. This coastal architecture is characterized by gabled wood-frame structures covered in cedar shingles (which could easily be replaced if damaged), set upon pile foundations embedded into the sand to allow for ocean overwash during times of unusually high tides and storm surges.

These houses have roots in both the villages of the Outer Banks and back on the farm, for the planters built what they knew. Though some academics might argue for a likeness to the Shingle style, the only similarities are in the use of exterior cladding and the unification of the main house and its dependencies, or subsidiary structures, under one extended roof. Design elements such as wraparound, single-story porches and breezeways connect the main house to its dependencies. Dormer windows in the upstairs bedrooms provide more space on the upper level. The wooden storm shutters and awnings that now appear as a decorative motif were a necessity in the old days. Cantilevered built-in porch benches are unique to the Old Nags Head idiom. Like hammocks, they contributed to the desirability of outdoor seating. The ground-level pilings were often wrapped in chicken wire, creating a makeshift stable for livestock and a barrier to the wild cattle that freely grazed the Outer Banks.

Two movements existed within Old Nags Head architecture.

The first was influenced by the existing structures in the region. In fact, it is not possible to discuss the Nags Head cottages built between the 1860s and the 1920s without describing the homes occupied by permanent residents of Corolla, Kitty Hawk, Rodanthe, Avon, Roanoke Island, Hatteras Island, and Ocracoke Island. These dwellings contributed as much to the architectural legacy of Old Nags Head as did the tobacco barns back home.

In many ways, the existing structures in the region represented an organic Outer Banks architecture in its purest form, the builders long forgotten, the parts sometimes salvaged from shipwrecks and structures destroyed by storms. Most of these dwellings appeared on what the locals called "the back side," or the sound side, of the barrier islands, which was where most year-round settlements were located, as was the initial the Old Nags Head colony. The sound side was protected from harsh northeast winds and damaging salt spray. The brackish water of Currituck and Roanoke Sounds was a fishery for flounder, striped bass, spot, croaker, and mullet. The muddy banks, rich in nutrients, were suitable for growing trees and shrubs for protection and vegetable gardens for sustenance. Most of the occupants of these sound-side hamlets were fishermen, hunters, farmers, and herders. They seined the sounds and the ocean for seafood, trapped and shot wild animals and waterfowl, grew produce in their side yards, and allowed their livestock to freely roam the islands. Many villagers were shipwreck victims who never left the area, while others were extended family members of lighthouse keepers and surfmen who moved to the Outer Banks to be near their loved ones.

Many of the early Old Nags Head homes derived from what is known as the "coastal cottage"—a single-gabled, single-story house with a varied roofline to compensate for a shed porch on the front elevation and an enclosed shed addition on the rear. These wood-frame coastal cottages were set upon brick piers and covered with weatherboards. The floor plan included a side hall and a parlor.

One variation of the coastal cottage was a one-and-a-half-story structure distinguished by a gabled roof interrupted by an extended dormer. The Old Nags Head version of this house was built of shingles over a wood frame. It was set upon wood pilings and had wraparound porches on the east, south, and west sides to benefit from sultry winds in summer. The shed enclosure was located on the north to protect the interior rooms from the prevailing northeast winds from late summer through early spring. As time went on, other additions were made to these cottages along the northwest elevation.

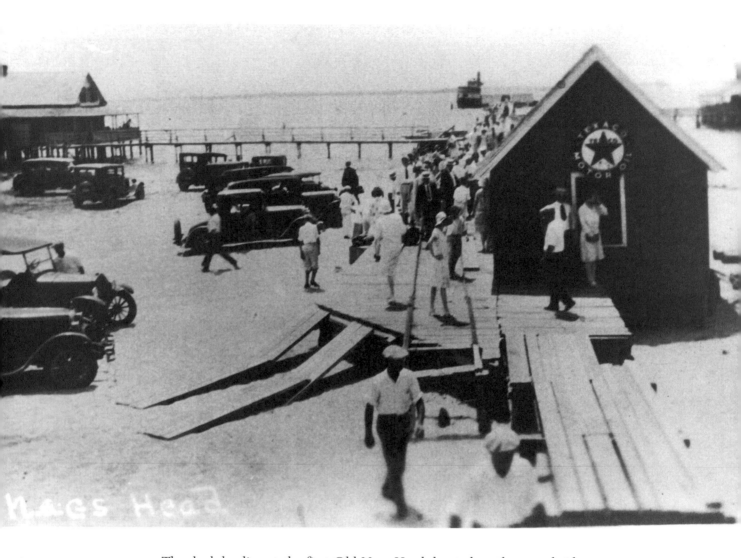

The dock landing at the first Old Nags Head, located on the sound side

Old Nags Head Soundside Home

While the coastal cottage dominated the vernacular architecture of the seaside villages, the I-house, a single-gabled, two-story dwelling, proliferated in the inland towns of the Albemarle. It was usually a wood-frame house finished with weatherboards. It was set upon brick piers and had a front shed-roof porch and an enclosed rear addition. When this pattern was adapted for Old Nags Head, the wood-frame house was set upon pilings and shingled. Again, porches wrapped around the east, south, and west elevations, and additions were made to the north and northwest elevations.

The third form that influenced the Old Nags Head style was the four-square cottage, which was arranged around a central hall under a hipped, bonnet roof. This cottage could easily be expanded from one story to two. It, too, was set upon pilings and had wraparound porches at the first level and extensions along the north and northwest elevations. The Outlaw Cottage, built in 1885, anchors Old Nags Head Beach Cottage Row and is a prime example of the hip-roofed form.

The second architectural movement that influenced Old Nags Head was a regional interpretation of the Arts and Crafts style of the 1920s, in which the bungalow was popularized in suburbs throughout America. Stephen J. Twine, an Elizabeth City builder, introduced the bungalow to the Old Nags Head community. Twine is the only builder who has received credit for the design and construction of any of the vintage Old Nags Head homes. His signature was in the massing of the cottages— which were four or five bays wide and two or three bays deep—under a gabled roof with extended dormers. His timber-framed exteriors were clad in cedar shingles or weatherboards. Of the sixty cottages listed in the National Register nomination, a dozen were Twine bungalows built between the early 1920s and the mid-1930s.

Some of the centerpieces of Old Nags Head have burned or been destroyed by storms. Both lifesaving stations at Nags Head were demolished during the Ash Wednesday Storm of 1962. The First Colony Inn, relocated away from the nucleus of Old Nags Head, has been refurbished and is still in use as a bed-and-breakfast. Nellie Myrtle Pridgen's general store stands at the corner of Soundside Road and Virginia Dare Trail, though it is open on special occasions only. St. Andrew's By-the-Sea Episcopal Church remains a vital part of Nags Head even today.

The Outlaw Cottage
1885

Anchoring Old Nags Head at its southern border is the old Outlaw place, erected in 1885. The Outlaws were among the first families of Nags Head. Their cottage, initially a single-story structure, is one of the thirteen original houses here. The Outlaw Cottage is a testament to its era. Its appearance is Spartan, unlike the others. It is four-square, not gabled, and it is clad in weatherboards, not cedar shakes. It has a hip roof with no dormers. There are no breezeways or extensions to soften the spare exterior. All of this belies the colorful history of its origins and its creator, Confederate captain Edward R. Outlaw.

Family members who summer here call the cottage "O 85." The first of Captain Outlaw's descendants to open the cottage each spring is obliged to raise the Confederate flag, a symbol of the pride that has been passed down from each generation to the next. There are many limbs to this family's tree, the roots of which begin near the eastern North Carolina town of Windsor in an area known as Indian Woods.

"O 85" was made from 150-foot pine trees that grew at Liberty Hall, the captain's 2,700-acre Indian Woods plantation. The plantation, once Tuscarora Indian land, bordered the Roanoke River. It was there, at a landing the Indians and the Outlaws called Quitsna, that the heart-pine timbers for "O 85" were loaded on a steamer headed for Old Nags Head. The captain's brother-in-law, Aaron Rascoe, contributed artifacts taken from the old Windsor Tavern, built during the 1830s. That roadhouse had recently been dismantled. According to family legend, Rascoe considered the doors and windows especially suited for the cottage at the beach.

Captain Outlaw and his hands boarded a steamer and traveled from Quitsna Landing across Albemarle Sound, arriving on the banks of Roanoke Sound at Nags Head. They unloaded the lumber and hauled it by horse and cart across the dunes to the home's present oceanfront site. Since the Outlaw Cottage was erected in 1885, it has been moved back from the Atlantic five times—a total of four hundred feet.

The single-story house was set upon pilings. The four-room floor plan was designed

Outlaw Cottage, c. 1885, original one-story structure

PHOTOGRAPH COURTESY OF OUTER BANKS HISTORY CENTER / WILLARD JONES POST CARD COLLECTION

SEASIDE. NAGS HEAD, N.C.

Outlaw Cottage (left) after second-story addition, c. 1900
PHOTOGRAPH COURTESY OF OUTER BANKS HISTORY CENTER / WILLARD JONES POST CARD COLLECTION

around a central hall and entrances at the east and west elevations. The outbuildings included a detached kitchen, servants' quarters, and a small stable for livestock. A second floor was added just after the turn of the twentieth century.

Today, the hip-roofed porch wraps around the first level. Benches have been carved out of the corner railings and cantilevered over the edge of the porch floor. Platform rockers face the ocean, and potted geraniums and begonias add a dash of color to the weathered, silver-gray exterior. When the cross-and-Bible doors from the old tavern are opened, sunlight brightens the dark-paneled interior. The walls are uninsulated and unfinished, and the plumbing and electrical systems are completely exposed. Several of the six bedrooms have authentic iron beds. The family still dines at the long wooden table where the captain and his family once sat.

According to Outlaw lore, the captain, though retired from the Confederate army, never traveled without his uniform, as he planned to be buried in it. And so he was, following the summer day in 1914 when he passed away in the front bedroom of "O 85."

The Winston Cottage
1866-1875

"This was the laziest place I was ever at," wrote M. E. Dunstan to her husband one Tuesday evening in August 1888. "We don't do anything much but eat and sleep and ride about." Mrs. Dunstan and her two sons, Henry and Fred, were guests of Mr. and Mrs. Duncan C. Winston, who bought this house in 1880.

The Winston Cottage is among the oldest on the beach at Old Nags Head, although the exact date of construction has not been confirmed. One source suggests the house was built in 1866 for Henrietta Fearing, but the current owner, Betty Wales Silver, Duncan Winston's great-granddaughter, believes it dates to around 1875.

In 1997, the Winston Cottage was moved back from the ocean and renovated by Silver's son, John. In order to do this, he removed the lower-level porches from the two-story, single-gabled house and its two-story extension. Altogether, there are three porches—one on the oceanfront, one on the south side, and one attached to the rear extension. Next, he removed the second-floor dormers, boarded the windows, and had the house jacked up off its pilings and transported one hundred feet west to its present site, where he commenced an extensive remodeling.

John Silver is more than a carpenter. He is an artist. His mother's cottage has been the site of his annual Thanksgiving weekend art show. The oceanfront living room, paneled in pine planks, is the perfect backdrop for his lively watercolors of age-old Nags Head beach scenes of bathers and fishermen. The watercolors glisten like bright bits of beach glass against the warm, sandy brown walls. Silver, who takes top prizes in the North Carolina Watercolor Society's exhibitions, makes his patrons feel like long-lost family friends. They stroll from living room to dining room, where the table is draped with lacy cloth, laid with heirloom silver, and dressed with a home-cooked holiday meal—turkey, cranberry sauce, ham biscuits, oatmeal cookies, lemon squares. The laughter and the tinkle of crystal transport the guests back to the days described by M. E. Dunstan in her letters home, as in this one to her sister: "We have had beautiful weather this summer and it has been very pleasant down here. I would be glad to have you with me and as father's health is improved and your turkies

gone, cotton crop done, I don't see why you can't come. I shall not stay here longer than three weeks more, I don't think and you must hurry and come down or you will not have anytime to stay. You had better go to Windsor next Thursday and come down on the *Lucy* Friday night, or you can go by E. City [Elizabeth City] and get here Saturday."

The Whedbee Cottage
1866

While many Old Nags Head residents have relinquished part of the past to modernize their homes, the owners of the Whedbee Cottage have made every attempt to maintain their beach house in an authentic state.

The two-story frame cottage, once located on the oceanfront, is believed to have been built in 1866 for Mrs. Kate Overman, then subsequently sold to the following in succession: H. C. Tunis, Tom Old, Charles Whedbee, and John Buchanan. After a hurricane in 1933, the Whedbees, of Hertford, moved the house away from the ocean and across Virginia Dare Trail, known locally as "the Beach Road," to its present location.

Old Nags Head Beach Cottage Row Historic District
PHOTOGRAPH BY DREW C. WILSON / COURTESY OF OUTER BANKS HISTORY CENTER

The cottage is three bays wide and has covered porches on all four sides with cantilevered benches attached to the balustrades. The original windows are held in place with wooden toggles. The wooden storm shutters are side-hinged on the first story and awning-hinged on the second story. There are three rooms on the first floor. The living room, to the right of the main entrance, faces east. Adjoining it on the north side is the dining room, which features a three-sided bay window. To the left of the main entrance are a bedroom and a stairway to the second floor, where there are two more bedrooms and a bath. A scarf joint connects the main house to the servants' quarters and the detached kitchen, which is equipped with antique artifacts such as an old ice chest and a vintage pine-board "beat'n biscuit" table.

The late Charles Whedbee was brought to this house as an infant. Whedbee enjoyed a long and distinguished career as an eastern North Carolina attorney and district-court judge. His boyhood in Old Nags Head always remained dear to him. In a 1987 interview in *Carolina Coast*, he told reporter Jon Glass that one of the principal nighttime entertainments in Old Nags Head was building a beach fire when there was an offshore breeze. People would sit around it and sing, then, when the embers died down, the older members of the group would begin to tell tales from their youth. Once Whedbee realized that the stories might die as the old-timers passed on, he felt the need to write them down and preserve them. His first book, *Legends of the Outer Banks and Tar Heel Tidewater*, published in 1966, is still a big seller after seventeen printings, and his other four collections of tales aren't far behind.

Frank Stick and the Southern Shores Flat Top

Southern Shores, the first planned, ocean-to-sound community on the Outer Banks, was the site of an architectural accident—the Flat Top. Such accidents occur when need collides with visionary genius. When the first Flat Top appeared in 1947, it pushed the limits of what had been considered acceptable up to that point.

Frank Stick studied art under Howard Pyle at the Brandywine School in Wilmington, Delaware. His paintings graced the covers of the *Saturday Evening Post, Field & Stream*, and the fiction of Zane Grey. A model named Maud Hayes was a frequent subject of his work, as well as that of his best friend and contemporary, William Koerner. Koerner's portrait of Hayes on the cover of a 1922 issue of the *Saturday Evening Post* launched the serialization of a story called "The Covered Wagon." From that time, Maud Hayes became known as "the Madonna of the Prairie." She also became Frank Stick's wife and the mother of his two children—a daughter, the late Charlotte Stick McMullan, and a son, David Stick, preeminent civic leader and historian of the Outer Banks.

After over six hundred illustrations, Frank

Aerial view of Ocean Boulevard in Southern Shores

PHOTOGRAPH BY B. J. NIXON / COURTESY OF OUTER BANKS HISTORY CENTER

Stick was ending his twenty-year career as a commercial artist when he first visited the Outer Banks in the early 1920s. Advances in photography and printing techniques were changing the look of mass-produced calendars, magazines, and books. Furthermore, America was ending its love affair with the pioneer, the roughrider, and the cowboy—images that figured prominently in Stick's work—and turning its heart over to a new cultural hero, the wealthy industrialist. Many of these moneyed privateers were coming to the Outer Banks to hunt and fish, and Stick was not far behind, visiting for a number of years before resettling his family here in 1929.

Stick became known locally as a conservationist and developer. His essays and lobbying efforts in the 1930s were instrumental in establishing three national-park facilities on the Outer Banks—Cape Hatteras National Seashore, the first national seashore park in the United States; Fort Raleigh National Historic Site on Roanoke Island, the site of the first English-speaking colony in the New World; and Wright Brothers National Memorial in Kill Devil Hills, which commemorates the first man-powered airplane flights in history.

Stick also sought legislation to prohibit the use of the Outer Banks as an open range for grazing livestock. As a real-estate speculator, he spent a decade—and every penny he had, according to his son—buying, selling, and trading options on property from Hatteras Island to Colington Island. During that time, he formed many partnerships and made numerous attempts to develop the oceanfront. One early effort resulted in Virginia Dare Shores, a community in Kill Devil Hills. A sound-side dock and two pavilions he built on Kitty Hawk Bay were destroyed by a hurricane, but not before the site served as a backdrop for the twenty-fifth anniversary of the Wright brothers' flights and hosted a banquet attended by Orville Wright and Amelia Earhart in 1932. In 1933, Stick designed a cluster of large, Cape Cod–style bungalows on the Kill Devil Hills oceanfront. Collectively, they came to be called Millionaires' Row. Several of those homes are still in use today.

After World War II, Stick acquired an option on a twenty-eight-hundred-acre tract north of Kitty Hawk for thirty thousand dollars. It was to be the largest ocean-to-sound parcel subdivided for single-family home sites

The McMullan Cottage, designed by David Stick, was built in 1948.

PHOTOGRAPH BY AYCOCK BROWN / COURTESY OF DAVID STICK COLLECTION

in local history. In a singular act of foresight, Stick called this community Southern Shores, even though it represented the northern frontier of real-estate development on the Outer Banks.

Phase I of Southern Shores opened in 1946 with fifty oceanfront building sites. Only one sale was made that first year. The success of Millionaires' Row had taught Stick that improved building sites sold more quickly than vacant lots. But lumber and other traditional building supplies were still reserved for government use, stalling the construction of new homes. Desperate to show a profit, Stick decided to build himself a house. In the process, he created a new vernacular architectural form: the Flat Top.

To help with the construction of his house, Stick lured Hatteras Islander Curtis Gray to Kitty Hawk. Together, they set up a factory in Kitty Hawk village for the manufacture of cement blocks—forty-two pounds each, made from local beach sand. These blocks were the principal material used to construct Flat Top cottages until the mid-1950s, when the North Carolina legislature banned the use of beach gravel for manufacturing concrete. The Flat Tops built between 1955 and 1965 were made from cinder blocks manufactured in eastern North Carolina.

The Flat Top was adapted for its barrier-island setting from the single-story, flat-roofed block houses of Florida. To those design elements, Stick added an extended overhang and a bright, whitewashed exterior. When combined, the two new features deflected the intense heat of the sun away from the house, so the interior remained cool in summer. Louvered doors and screened windows encouraged the flow of the prevailing southerly winds. The exposed soffits and storm shutters were painted in brilliant shades of crimson, jade, emerald, and sapphire, introducing color to an otherwise monochromatic Outer Banks landscape.

The Southern Shores Flat Top was simply built. Before the foundation was poured, plumbing and drain lines were buried in the sand, then sealed with a concrete slab. Cement blocks were arranged around the periphery up to floor-level elevation. More blocks were added to make the walls, up to twelve courses high. A Flat Top house took roughly four months to build and cost one-third less than a traditional home.

By 1948, the postwar economy was steadily trickling dollars into the pockets of middle-class families, who now enjoyed the mobility associated with owning an automobile. Possessing a seaside vacation home—a privilege once reserved for the wealthy elite—was suddenly a possibility.

Like the founders of the Bauhaus school of design in Germany in the 1920s, Frank Stick overturned conventional architectural styles and used nontraditional materials to execute his house plans. Like Frank Lloyd Wright's Prairie-style homes, Stick's Flat Tops were an organic form. They reiterated the surrounding environment and emphasized wide-open spaces in horizontal planes that blended with bands of sky and sea. Furthermore, Stick's Flat Tops were second homes made in the likeness of Wright's more practical Usonian homes, which were designed so middle-income families could enjoy the same amenities as wealthier clients.

As the real-estate market fluctuated, site plans for Southern Shores were made, discarded, adopted, and abandoned during the early years of the community. Fifty-foot-wide oceanfront lots were surveyed and platted. They were sold in pairs for two thousand dollars, with a 10 percent discount if a house was built within six months. The Flat Tops became the predominant local form. They remained popular through the 1960s, reaching their zenith as a stylistic idiom around 1965.

Once the Flat Top movement was under way, Frank Stick built himself a one-room art studio. Even though he had put down his brushes and vowed never again to paint for profit, he rendered pen-and-ink sketches to illustrate his son's book *Graveyard of the Atlantic*, published in 1952. In 1955, he retired from his real-estate dealings and returned to painting. He and his wife traveled to Waverly Mills, South Carolina, San Carlos Bay, Florida, and eventually Key West. The work he produced during that time—mostly maritime scenes—is part of the permanent collection at the Outer Banks History Center in Manteo. Those paintings evoke the work of Brandywine School classmates like N. C. Wyeth and contemporaries like Winslow Homer. Stick's final *oeuvre* was a watercolor series of magnificent Outer Banks sport fish. Those paintings were collected between the covers of *An Artist's Catch*, published posthumously in 1981.

In addition to resuming his painting, Stick took up the conservation cause, teaming with Laurence Rockefeller and others to establish a national park on St. John in the Virgin Islands

in 1965. Southern Shores, the Outer Banks town he created, was incorporated in 1974. It is the gateway to beach communities in Duck and Corolla to the north and a model for upscale residential resorts like Sanderling, Pine Island, the Currituck Club, and Corolla Light.

Today, more than fifty years after the first Flat Tops appeared on the oceanfront in Southern Shores, their number has dwindled. Their property values, which run consistent with the current real-estate market, range from $250,000 to $350,000. However, appraisals run little more than $50,000 for the vintage structures themselves.

Year by year, the water line at mean high tide inches closer and closer to the Flat Tops. Time will tell whether the man-made protective dunes erected in the 1930s by the Civilian Conservation Corps will slow the encroaching sea. Fortunately, the Southern Shores oceanfront is considered by geologists to be one of the more stable Outer Banks beaches. And at forty-two pounds per block, the Flat Tops are not likely to be going anywhere for some years to come.

The biggest threat to this indigenous Outer Banks architectural form is popular cultural values, as reflected in current building codes.

These include a Southern Shores town limit on renovation costs that restricts remodeling budgets to 50 percent of the value of the house. Since their plumbing and drain lines are buried under the foundations, the Flat Tops are a costly challenge to upgrade. Furthermore, building codes have been amended to minimize the damage from hurricanes and nor'easters, and all new homes—along with any additions to Flat Top cottages—must be elevated at least twenty feet. Today's tourists demand more amenities from their vacation houses than they can afford in their permanent homes. Therefore, resort properties are large and lavish. These new homes not only cost more to build, they also support large gatherings of extended families and friends to help defray weekly rental costs, thereby eliminating the need for single-family summer homes altogether. For these reasons, many realtors and contractors encourage buyers to demolish the old Flat Tops, especially since their generously proportioned oceanfront lots are suitable for much larger homes.

Fortunately, some of the authentic Flat Tops remain. Three of the first five built survive today. They are Frank Stick's own house (the Stick-Miller Home), the Taylor-Smith-Covington Cottage, and the Graves Cottage. Two of the old Flat Tops—the Graves Cottage and the Pipkin Cottage—are owned by members of the original families. In the past decade, as many as a half-dozen other Flat Tops have been judiciously restored.

The Stick-Miller Home (left) and The Huntington Cairns Cottage, built in 1948 (right)
Frank Stick and his studio are on the right in the foreground.

PHOTOGRAPH BY AYCOCK BROWN / COURTESY OF DAVID STICK COLLECTION

The First Southern Shores Flat Top
<u>The Stick-Miller Home</u>
1947

Frank Stick paved the first road in Southern Shores in 1947 and set his house equidistant between the street he named Ocean Boulevard and the Atlantic. Even though the protective dunes erected in 1933 prohibited views of the sea from the one-story block cottage, there was no muffling the roar of the surf.

The floor plan for Stick's Flat Top became a blueprint for scores of others built between 1948 and 1965. It featured a central living room with a twelve-foot ceiling and a fireplace on the west wall. The ceiling dropped to eight feet where a screened porch adjoined the living area along the east elevation. North of the living room were the kitchen and the dining room. A master bedroom—added later at the northwest corner—functioned for a time as a studio. Three additional bedrooms and a bath were located on the south side of the house, as was an attached garage. Stick whitewashed his house and trimmed the exposed soffits and storm shutters a deep forest green.

Stick's house had a multilevel roofline that was intended to vary the interior ceiling heights. But the leaks that developed at each intersection caused this motif to be abandoned. One central raked roof became the pattern with subsequent Flat Tops.

The home also had exterior accent walls that balanced the bulkiness of the block cottage. These exterior facades became part of the Flat Top idiom in future construction. Evidently, Stick added the walls sometime after the house was built, for they were made of cinder block and not cement. They appeared as low masonry walls and an arched doorway that hid yard tools and garbage cans and also screened a walkway from the kitchen door to the porch. At the southeast corner was a low, L-shaped wall that marked a footpath to a neighbor's house.

Frank Stick occupied his Flat Top cottage at 60 Ocean Boulevard until he passed away in 1966. Maud, his wife, continued to live in the house until her death in 1973. Today, the Miller family of Warrenton, Virginia, owns Frank Stick's Flat Top, which remains little changed since his time. A new hot-water heater, a new kitchen stove, and a microwave are the only modest improvements. The leaks are authentic, as are the sloped ceilings, the curved walls, the lantern in the dining room, the Chinese red countertops, and the kitchen cabinets made by Kitty Hawk carpenters Charlie Spruill and Arnold Perry.

"Portsmouth Tide"
The Graves Cottage
1948

When Grandmother Graves came to the Outer Banks to fish in the spring and fall, she made many friends among the locals. Her son, Edward Spencer Graves, built a cottage for her in 1948. It was an atypical Flat Top—two stories high, with room enough to accommodate the constant parade of houseguests from the family's hometown of Lynchburg, Virginia. According to Edward S. Graves II, the youngest of Grandmother Graves's seventeen grandchildren, she wanted a big house so that she could bring her entire Sunday school to visit. There was always a group coming down to use the cottage a week at a time every spring and fall. First, the men of the church would come down to fish. Then the ladies would come to play bridge. Then the women would come down a few weeks later to fish, followed by the men, who would come to play bridge. Even though the tradition has declined in recent years, trophies with engraved brass plaques awarded to the victors of those fishing and card-playing marathons line the bookshelves of the cottage today.

The first floor included a living room, a dining room, a kitchen, a screened porch, Grandmother Graves's suite, and another suite for the family cook. The second floor was balanced on either side by two large, open decks. Uncle Edward's room adjoined "the grownups' porch," while the bunk room at the top of the stairs and a guest room adjoined "the children's porch."

The house rules, posted in the kitchen, began with this from Gilbert and Sullivan's *HMS Pinafore*: "When at anchor we ride, on the Portsmouth Tide, we have plenty of time to play." When the family's children were deemed old enough to begin helping out around the place, they were anointed into stewardship aboard the family cottage, Portsmouth Tide. Young Edward Graves II was ten or eleven when he received instructions on how to mix cocktails for his elders. He would subsequently be summoned from the children's porch to the grownups' porch and given drink orders. He then prepared the beverages in the "fanny kitchen," so named because it was so narrow that everyone bumped fannies when they walked through it. The elders' drinks frequently required freshening up, so there was much hollering back and forth between porches and a lot of running up and down the stairs. Even now, not-so-young-anymore Edward can proudly recite his steward's motto, "Wait, serve, and look after others," which he did for nearly twenty years before he was invited to join the adults.

It should come as no surprise to learn that the Graves Cottage was the social nucleus of a cluster of oceanfront cottages owned mainly by families from Lynchburg. The homes were known collectively as "the Compound." To the north were the homes of Vernon Giles and James Watts. To the south were those of Peter Dunne, Frank Stick, and Huntington Cairns.

The late Betsy Giles best described the perpetual party that went on at the isolated beach in those days. She told a story of how, one evening, a female member of the Graves family was walking along the beach when she met Huntington Cairns's mother. Mrs. Cairns supposedly remarked, "My son is fascinated by what goes on at your house every night," to which Mrs. Graves replied, "The children are playing kick the can. Tell your little boy to come over." And sure enough, forty-something Huntington Cairns, who was then the chief legal counsel for the National Gallery of Art in Washington, came over that night to play kick the can with the children. Betsy Giles howled with laughter in remembering.

Another habitué of "the Compound" was Finley Peter Dunne, son of the author of *Doctor Dolittle*. Finley Peter Dunne was a poet himself, as well as a Capitol Hill lobbyist for the Presbyterian Church. Edward Graves II re-members many lively conversations during cocktail hour, especially the perennial debate between Cairns and Dunne in which Cairns argued that there was too much religion in politics.

Another noteworthy personality was Henrietta Hoopes Heath, a renegade socialite from Wilmington, Delaware, who had disgraced her family by running off to Paris to study painting instead of coming out. Henrietta was a contemporary of Frank Stick's, and the two often shared top billing at the Delaware Art Museum's annual exhibitions. Her portrait of Huntington Cairns is part of the permanent collection in the National Portrait Gallery in Washington.

It's no wonder that Edward Graves II relishes his grandmother's old cottage while simultaneously lamenting the constant maintenance required to keep it up. Even though many neighbors sold their oceanfront property when the elders passed on—fetching more than ten times the initial investment—Graves remains steadfast. Put simply, the house has too many memories and so much character.

"Craving Nostalgia"
The Taylor-Smith-Covington Cottage
1947

Bat Taylor, an aviator, and his wife, Marian, an artist, built a Flat Top on the oceanfront in Southern Shores in 1947. It was one of a handful of block cottages designed by David Stick, the son of Frank Stick, who succeeded his father as developer of Southern Shores from 1956 to 1976.

David Stick's design for the house followed his father's template for a central living room. But from there, the floor plan flip-flopped. The kitchen was placed at the southwest corner, instead of the northeast, and the bedrooms were located in the north wing, instead of the south. The most unusual element was the crescent-shaped hearth tucked into the northeast corner of the living room. On the property's north side was a detached wing that served as the maid's room and a garage.

Fifty years after the Taylors' house was built, Joe and Janet Covington bought it from Malcolm Smith for $385,000. They initially planned to demolish the cottage, but after spending one night in it, they began considering an extensive restoration that would spare one of the last authentic Flat Tops. It reminded them of the old places in South Beach, Florida. When the Covingtons discovered the guest book, they learned that several families had reared their children at the cottage. The pages were inscribed with soft-hearted messages such as this: "To the new owners—we love the place, please don't change it." The Covingtons felt a responsibility to uphold those memories and accept the challenge of sensitively remodeling a home that had so much charm and so much appeal the way it was.

Fortunately, they were no strangers to the renovation process, having teamed up on many projects during their years of running their own construction and plumbing firm in Hampton Roads, Virginia.

Like other Flat Top owners, the Covingtons were restricted by town building codes that limited the cost of renovations to 50 percent of the value of the structure. In their case, the cottage itself was worth fifty thousand dollars. By dividing the project into phases, however, they were able to spend twenty-five thousand the first year and an additional twenty-five

The Sellers Cottage, designed by Frank Stick, was built in 1949.

thousand the second year to achieve their re-modeling goals.

The Covingtons considered a renovation plan that would have linked the modest guest wing to the main house on the northeast corner. However, the flood line ran through the center of their living room. Therefore, any additions to the house needed to be twenty feet above the mean high-tide line (allowing for an eighteen-foot storm surge, plus two additional feet), with no ground-level obstructions. Such an addition would have disrupted the lines of the house and destroyed its authenticity.

Because they couldn't expand, Janet Covington, an interior designer, decided to furnish the house like a well-appointed, classic yacht, using built-in cabinets and a minimum of loose furniture. She succeeded in meeting the demands of today's rental market while choosing finishes and fixtures that the couple wanted for themselves. The result was a blend of old and new, vintage and contemporary—an eclectic, harmonious mix of textures and styles.

In the fall of 1997, the first phase of renovations began in the two-bedroom, two-bath guest wing. The plumbing and electrical systems were upgraded. The original white cedar paneling was carefully removed and replaced with white drywall, after which the cedar was given a second life when the boards were used to construct built-in vanity cupboards and bedroom bureaus. Berber carpet, granite countertops, and new bathroom fixtures were added, and the window sills and doorframes were refinished.

Restoration of the main house began in the winter of 1998, when Joe Covington and his crew dug a trench across the concrete-slab floor to improve the kitchen and bathroom plumbing. Once again, drywall was installed and the original wallboards were harvested and transformed, this time into a built-in entertainment center and bookshelves in the living room. The entire east elevation was raised two feet, and all of the windows were replaced. New appliances arrived for the kitchen by the spring of 1999, but the original wooden icebox and the countertop built by Charlie Spruill and Arnold Perry remained intact. The interior entrance to the screened porch was moved to make space for a dining room. The guest room and bath were rehabilitated. And the master bedroom suite, which was semiprivate, was made exclusive.

Today, the quality of these interior spaces

is enhanced by "outdoor rooms"—a vintage 1950s shuffleboard court, a walled seaside garden, and a sixteen-by-thirty-two-foot lap pool and terrace—framed by low stone walls with glass-block details. Windows throughout the house extend the yacht metaphor and invite these "outdoor rooms" indoors.

The Covingtons rent their house for ten weeks out of the prime summer season. But from mid-August to late May, they spend as much time as possible at Craving Nostalgia. The first thing they do is grab the guest book. They are frequently gratified by the comments. Everyone raves about the place. The Covingtons' meticulous restoration is in perfect pitch with the entry made by John and Becky Quann on July 19, 1997, and read by the Covingtons on their first, fateful night in the cottage: "Anything less would have been roughing it, anything more would have been too stuffy."

"Barefoot Elegance"
The Smith-Millican-Garrett Home
1950

"The purple martins left four days ago, but they'll be back," laughs Ben Garrett, standing beside an assortment of birdhouses in the front yard of his lavish Flat Top cottage.

Barefoot Elegance, the home at 100 Ocean Boulevard, was built in 1950 by Brad and Ruth Smith. It was extensively remodeled forty years later by Ted and Marylou Millican. Ben and Dee Garrett now own the Flat Top, as well as a property-management firm specializing in high-end vacation rentals.

The Garretts and Bob de Gabrielle bought the house in 1994 with the idea of leasing it as a vacation property. In 1997, the Garretts bought de Gabrielle's share and took the house over. The following year, the couple tried living in the place for the winter, gradually transferring their personal effects from their Nags Head home to Southern Shores. They fell in love with the cottage and decided to stay permanently.

The original floor plan had a central living room balanced by two wings. The north wing

The Haserot Cottage, designed by David Stick and built in 1948, was demolished in 1998.

PHOTOGRAPH BY AYCOCK BROWN / COURTESY OF DAVID STICK COLLECTION

housed a master bedroom suite on the west side and a kitchen facing east. The south wing had two guest rooms and a bath. A screened porch wrapped the southeast corner. A separate apartment connected to the detached garage originally accommodated domestic staff in the 1950s. It was converted into guest quarters during the 1960s.

Architectural designer Jude LeBlanc drew the plans for the 1990 renovation, which included a substantial addition that doubled the square footage as well as the interior elevation. Without disrupting the living space, LeBlanc blew the roof off the east wall and created a central atrium filled with tropical house plants. The addition included a contemporary, open kitchen and dining area, plus a Florida-style sunroom and a wet bar. Through the selection of interior finishes, the old was blended with the new. Glass-block walls linked the original living room to the atrium. All of the exterior walls were stucco and the roof tiles terra cotta, which served to unify the house and its dependencies. The construction of another garage along the south edge of the property helped put the outbuildings and the main structure in balance. Low concrete walls—one forming a courtyard near the front entrance and surrounding an indoor lap pool, the other flanking the roadway—extended the villa theme common to island settings and supported a level of privacy not usually found along Ocean Boulevard in Southern Shores. Today, the Mediterranean flavor distinguishes this house from all the rest.

The Garretts have perpetuated a decorative tradition handed down from one owner to the next. From a halyard on the ocean side, the original owners, the Smiths, raised as many as three or four flags at a time from their extensive collection; the flags were those of the countries that were in the news that day. The Smiths also created a series of steppingstones that led from the porch door to the beach. Each concrete rectangle was embedded with beach glass and seashells arranged into familiar icons—a crab, a sailboat, a candle, a Carolina Tar Heel. From those homemade stones, the second owners, Ted and Marylou Millican, selected the Tar Heel as the emblem for their house, Barefoot Elegance. They incorporated the symbol into the design of a house flag—a pair of hot-pink bare feet blazing inside a circle of green that floats across a sky-blue field. The flag occasionally waves in the sea breeze today.

"The Pink House"
The Roth Cottage
1950s

Hot-pink cement blocks, exposed dovetail soffits, raised storm shutters, and louvered doors decorate the exterior of this Flat Top like frosting on a wedding cake. Inside, the pastel walls of the Pink House light up like a rainbow as the sun makes its arc across the sky.

Slender rays peek through tobacco-brown Plantation blinds in the living room. The exposed walnut-stained beams and the bare, uninsulated juniper ceiling contrast with the pale yellow stone walls. Bentwood rattan, four canes wide, frames the cushioned sofa and the oval swivel chair perched on a round rattan base. The bamboo end tables have a triangular shape, while the oversized, glass-topped coffee table is square. The suite of furniture faces the fireplace on the south wall, which is made of red bricks horizontally laid. In the niches are a pair of urns and in the corner a rattan teacart, a sink, and a large watercolor in which palm trees flank a dark-skinned man in a sombrero who is riding a donkey across the horizon.

In the northeast ell is the dining room. The kitchen, a vibrant robin's-egg blue, is a brilliant contrast to the master bedroom it adjoins, which is painted pink. The bedroom and its private bath occupy the entire northwest-southeast axis, so as to benefit from the prevailing southwesterly winds in summer. In the south wing, three guest rooms painted varying shades of sea green share a bath. The screened porch attached to the east elevation is buffered by the dunes from the breakers beyond.

Barbara Roth and her husband, Lieutenant Colonel Martin E. Roth, came to the Outer Banks in 1963, after the Ash Wednesday Storm of 1962, to look around for something to buy. For twenty-five thousand dollars, they ended up with this Flat Top and everything that came with it—from the lawn buoy in the front yard to the monogrammed towels in the master bath to the 150 feet of prime oceanfront real estate. Barbara Roth made only two alterations, changing the exterior color from an ugly green

"The Pink House," also known as The Roth Cottage, c. 1955

to pink and adding a pair of kitchen cupboards with shelves tall enough for a large gin bottle.

"Pink Perfection"
The Pipkin Cottage
1953

"There's nowhere such comfort, we think, as at Pipkin's Perfection in Pink. There's nothing lugubrious, all is salubrious. Good Talk, Good Food and Good Drink," wrote houseguest William McKinley Eden on July 13, 1974.

It's true. Pink Perfection is the epitome of a vintage Flat Top. It is one of only two architect-designed structures built along Ocean Boulevard in the 1950s, and the last one owned by members of its original family.

In 1951, Emily Edith Pipkin purchased two adjoining oceanfront lots from Frank Stick for twenty-eight hundred dollars. Miss Edith was a schoolteacher and the corporate secretary for her family's business, the Cone Cotton Mill in Reidsville, North Carolina. She hired Edward Lowenstein, an architect from Greensboro, to design a summer house for herself, her brother,

his family, and their friends. The Kitty Hawk firm of Spruill and Perry completed the home in 1953 at a cost of twenty-six thousand dollars. Miss Edith named the house Pink Perfection, after her favorite camellia, and had the exterior walls painted pink and the storm shutters and soffits painted a leafy green.

The living-room entrance adjoined a screened porch that extended across the east side of the house. Three bedrooms lined up along the northwest-southeast axis to benefit from the prevailing southwesterly winds during summer. These bedrooms had transom windows along the interior walls to regulate the flow of air from the corridor, which also adjoined the screened porch. The kitchen occupied the northeast corner of the house, as did the service wing, which included a maid's suite and a small apartment for Miss Edith's chauffeur. Much of the cottage's original furniture—the dining and coffee tables, the chests of drawers, a desk, bookshelves, and custom cabinets for the master suite and the kitchen—are still in use today. The floors throughout were black and white linoleum tile. The stone walls were aquamarine and the kitchen counters Chinese red.

In 1957, Miss Edith purchased an additional pair of lots for another twenty-eight hundred dollars. When she died at sea on a cruise to Bermuda in 1971, Pink Perfection and the adjoining property passed to her younger brother, Willis Benton Pipkin, and his two sons, John Benton Pipkin and Ashmead Pringle Pipkin. Both Pipkin boys had vacationed in Southern Shores since they were teenagers. Driving John's Jeep, they had joined their contemporaries Billy Giles and Skipper Taylor, who also had Jeeps, to go scavenging the beaches for treasures like the flagpole, the boat ring, the cottage door, hatch covers, and other Outer Banks artifacts still in use at the cottage today.

In 1993, the family arrived at a crossroads—Pink Perfection had to grow or go. At the time, the property was appraised at just over half a million dollars, but the house itself was valued at a mere sixty thousand. Since the town of Southern Shores allowed only 50 percent of a home's value to be invested in renovations, the Pipkin brothers considered razing Aunt Edith's cottage, since its two oceanfront lots would support a much larger, more modern house for their growing families. But after searching their hearts, they arrived at a happy ending. They converted the chauffeur's quarters and the maid's room into a separate wing with its own entrance, a foyer, a guest room, a full bath, and a master bedroom suite, complete with central air conditioning and heat.

The changes were seamless, and the overall appearance of the house was not altered significantly. In fact, the description of Pink Perfection offered by North Carolina author T. R. Pearson in "When We Used to Go Where We Went," his autobiographical short story about boyhood summer vacations in Southern Shores, is still valid: "It was long and was low, but hardly troublesome to spy out on account of it was pink too, lively pink and in a spot where there was not anything else remotely pink at all."

"Pink Perfection," also known as The Pipkin Cottage, was designed by Edward Lowenstein and built in 1953.
PHOTOGRAPH BY AYCOCK BROWN / COURTESY OF DAVID STICK COLLECTION

North Carolina's Lifesaving Stations: Where Are They Now?

Author's Note: The status of lifesaving stations is occasionally difficult to determine because the Coast Guard sometimes sold the old stations, but not the land under them. Frequently, the stations that remained government surplus were moved from place to place and put into dry dock, as if they were ships in a harbor.

Station	Original/ Replacement	Location	Year Established	Architectural Style	Status
Wash Woods	Original station	Near Virginia line	1878	1876	Destroyed
Wash Woods	Replacement station	Wash Woods	1919	Chatham	Rental cottage
Penneys Hill	Original station	North of Currituck Light	1878	1876	Burned in 1970s
*Currituck Beach	Original station	Originally oceanfront opposite Currituck Light	1874	Chandler	Dismantled
Currituck Beach	Replacement station	Moved to Penneys Hill site	1903	Quonochontaug	Private home
Poyner's Hill	Original station	Moved to Corolla	1878	1876	Burned in 1989
Poyner's Hill	Replacement station	Ocean Sands	1913	Chicamacomico	Burned in 1970s
*Caffey's Inlet	Original station	Sanderling, north of Duck	1874	Chandler	Destroyed
Caffey's Inlet	Replacement station	Sanderling, north of Duck	1899	Quonochontaug	Restaurant
Paul Gamiels Hill	Original station	Duck	1878	1876	Burned
*Kitty Hawk	Original station	Milepost 4½	1874	Chandler	Restaurant
Kitty Hawk	Replacement station	Va. Dare Trail (Beach Rd.)	1911	Chicamacomico	Rental cottage

Station	Original/Replacement	Location	Year Established	Architectural Style	Status
Kill Devil Hills	Original station	Moved to Corolla; located on west side of N.C. 12, near Currituck Light	1878	1876	Retail shop
Kill Devil Hills	Replacement station	Located at milepost 8½ on the Va. Dare Trail	1933	U.S. Coast Guard	Private home
Nags Head	Original station	Milepost 12½	1874	Chandler	Destroyed in 1890
Nags Head	Replacement station	Va. Dare Trail (Beach Rd.)	1912	Chicamacomico	Destroyed in 1962
Bodie Island	Original station	Near Coquina Beach, on east side of N.C. 12	1878-79	1876	Owned by National Park Service
Bodie Island	Replacement station	Near Coquina Beach, on east side of N.C. 12	1925	Chatham	Owned by National Park Service
Oregon Inlet	Original station	Mouth of Oregon Inlet	1874	Chandler	Destroyed in 1897
Oregon Inlet	Replacement station	Mouth of Oregon Inlet	1897-98	Quonochontaug	Owned by Dare County
Pea Island	Original station	South of Oregon Inlet	1878-79	1876	Burned in 1880
Pea Island	Replacement station	Moved to Salvo, located on west side of N.C. 12	Rebuilt in 1881	1876	Retail shop
New Inlet	Original station	South of Pea Island	1882	1882	Destroyed, never rebuilt
Chicamacomico	Original station	Rodanthe, located on east side of N.C. 12	1874	Chandler	Owned by Chicamacomico Historical Association
Chicamacomico	Replacement station	Rodanthe, located on east side of N.C. 12	1911	Chicamacomico	Owned by Chicamacomico Historial Association

Station	Original/ Replacement	Location	Year Established	Architectural Style	Status
Gull Shoal	Original station	Salvo	1878	1876	Destroyed by hurricane in 1944
Little Kinnekeet	Original station	North of Avon	1874	Chandler	Owned by National Park Service
Little Kinnekeet	Replacement station	North of Avon	1904	Southern Pattern	Owned by National Park Service
Big Kinnekeet	Original station	Avon	1878	1876	Unknown
Big Kinnekeet	Replacement station	Avon	1929	Chatham	Damaged in 1944; later demolished
Cape Hatteras	Original station	Buxton	1882	1882	Demolished in 1930s
Creeds Hill	Original station	Frisco	1878	1876	Destroyed
Creeds Hill	Replacement station	Frisco	1918	Chatham	Owned by National Park Service
Durant Station	Original station	Hatteras	1878-79	1876	Rental cottage
Hatteras Inlet	Original station	North bank of Hatteras Inlet	1882	1882	Destroyed
Hatteras Inlet	Replacement station	South bank of Hatteras Inlet	1917	Chatham	Destroyed in 1955
Ocracoke	Original station	Ocracoke Island	1882-83	1882	Unknown
Ocracoke	Replacement station	Ocracoke Island	1904	Southern Pattern	Dismantled in 1940

Station	Original/ Replacement	Location	Year Established	Architectural Style	Status
Portsmouth Island	Original station	Portsmouth Island	1894	Quonochontaug	Owned by National Park Service
Core Banks	Original station	Atlantic Beach	1894	Quonochontaug	Burned
Cape Lookout	Original station	Harkers Island	1887	1882	Dismantled in 1940
Cape Lookout	Replacement station	Harkers Island	1916	Chatham	Owned by U.S. Coast Guard
Fort Macon	Original station	Beaufort	1904	Southern Pattern	Demolished or dismantled in 1950s or 1960s
Bogue Inlet	Original station	Originally located in Swansboro, moved to Cape Carteret	1904	Quonochontaug	Private home
Cape Fear	Original station	Smith Island, near Southport	1881-82	1882	Unknown
Cape Fear	Replacement station	Smith Island, near Southport	1918	Chatham	Unknown
Oak Island	Original station	West side of Cape Fear River	1888-89	1882	Unknown

*Denotes one of the original North Carolina Lifesaving Stations

Bibliography

Arnaudin, Steven. "North Carolina Coastal Vernacular." In *Carolina Dwelling*. Vol. 26. Raleigh: North Carolina State University School of Design, 1978.

Bisher, Catherine W. *Architects and Builders in North Carolina: A History of the Practice of Building*. Chapel Hill: University of North Carolina Press, 1990.

————. "The 'Unpainted Aristocracy': The Beach Cottages of Old Nags Head." *North Carolina Historical Review* 54 (October 1977).

Brimley, H. H. "Old Times on Currituck Sound." In *Wildlife in North Carolina*, edited by Jim Dean and Lawrence S. Early. Chapel Hill: University of North Carolina Press, 1987.

Conoley, William Neal. *Waterfowl Heritage*. Wendell, N.C.: Webfoot, Inc., 1982.

Cotter, Michael, editor. *Architectural Heritage of Greenville, North Carolina*. Greenville Area Preservation Association, 1988.

Dudley, Jack. *Carteret Waterfowl Heritage*. Morehead City, N.C.: Coastal Heritage Series.

Dunbar, Gary S. "The Banks in the Modern Era, 1865–1955." In *Historical Geography of the North Carolina Outer Banks*. Baton Rouge: Louisiana State University Press, 1958.

Early, Lawrence S. "Currituck Historic Sporting Clubs." In *Wildlife in North Carolina*, edited by Jim Dean and Lawrence S. Early. Chapel Hill: University of North Carolina Press, 1987.

Edwards, Jenny. *To Illuminate the Dark Space: Oral Histories of the Currituck Beach Lighthouse*. Corolla, N.C.: Outer Banks Conservationists, Inc., 1999.

Forbes, Carlin. "Waterfowl Hunting." In *Local History: The Heritage of Currituck County, North Carolina, 1670–1985*. Currituck County Historical Society, 1985.

Havemeyer, Frederick C., II. "Currituck Sound." In *Duck Shooting along the Atlantic Tidewater*, edited by Eugene V. Connett. William Morrow and Company, 1947.

Holland, Francis Ross, Jr. "A History of the Bodie Island Light Station." National Park Service, U.S. Department of the Interior, 1967. On file at Cape Hatteras National Seashore headquarters.

————. "Keeper's Dwelling, Cape Hatteras Light Station: Historic Structure Report,

Part 1." National Park Service, U.S. Department of the Interior, 1968. On file at Cape Hatteras National Seashore headquarters.

Johnson, Archie, and Bud Coppage. *Gun Clubs and Decoys of Back Bay and Currituck Sound*. Virginia Beach, Va.: CurBac Press, 1991.

McClure, Wesley A., et al. "Architecture of the Outer Banks." In *Design Manual: Cape Hatteras National Seashore, North Carolina*. Raleigh, N.C.: MTMA Design Group.

Mobley, Joe A. *Ship Ashore: The U.S. Lifesavers of Coastal North Carolina*. Raleigh: N.C. Department of Cultural Resources, Division of Archives and History, 1994.

National Register of Historic Places Nomination: Bodie Island Lighthouse Station. On file at Eastern Office (Greenville), North Carolina Division of Archives and History.

National Register of Historic Places Nomination: Cape Hatteras Lighthouse Station. On file at Eastern Office (Greenville), North Carolina Division of Archives and History.

National Register of Historic Places Nomination: Chicamacomico Lifesaving Station. On file at Eastern Office (Greenville), North Carolina Division of Archives and History.

National Register of Historic Places Nomination: Currituck Beach Lighthouse Station. On file at Eastern Office (Greenville), North Carolina Division of Archives and History.

National Register of Historic Places Nomination: Currituck Shooting Club. On file at Eastern Office (Greenville), North Carolina Division of Archives and History.

National Register of Historic Places Nomination: Ocracoke Lighthouse Station. On file at Eastern Office (Greenville), North Carolina Division of Archives and History.

National Register of Historic Places Nomination: Whalehead Club. On file at Eastern Office (Greenville), North Carolina Division of Archives and History.

Outlaw, Edward R., Jr. *Old Nags Head*, 1952.

Ruffin, Edmund. *Agricultural, Geological and Descriptive Sketches of Lower North Carolina and the Similar Adjacent Lands*. Raleigh, N.C.: Institute for the Deaf, Dumb and Blind, 1861.

Russell, Samuel. *History and Notes Relating to the Currituck Shooting Club*. Pelton and

King, Publishers, 1925.

Scully, Vincent J., Jr. *The Shingle Style and the Stick Style*. New Haven and London: Yale University Press, 1955.

Shanks, Ralph and Wick York. *The U.S. Life-Saving Service*. Petaluma, California: Costano Books, 1996.

Stick, David. *Graveyard of the Atlantic*. Chapel Hill: University of North Carolina Press, 1952.

————. *The Outer Banks of North Carolina*. Chapel Hill: University of North Carolina Press, 1958.

Tate, Elizabeth. "The Life Saving Service." In *Local History: The Heritage of Currituck County, North Carolina, 1670–1985*. Currituck County Historical Society, 1985.

Williamson, Clifford. *Unsung Heroes of the Surf*. Marshallburg, N.C.: Grandma Publications, 1992.

Wilson, John F., IV. "Conservation of Place: The Outer Banks of North Carolina." Master's thesis, George Washington University, 1981.

Glossary of Architectural Terms

Art Deco—a style of decorative art that began in the mid-1920s and became popular in the 1930s. Characteristic design details include floral motifs; repetitive geometric patterns, such as angles and circles; and, most notably, glass blocks.

Art Nouveau—a decorative arts movement that spanned the late 1890s and early 1900s. It is characterized by the irregular, curvilinear forms found in nature. These patterns are inspired by human, insect, and plant forms.

Arts and Crafts Movement—a movement initiated by English architects John Ruskin and William Morris. It emphasized hand-built, custom-designed finishes and furnishings and cabinets made from natural materials.

Bay—a term used for a unit or open space within a building, such as a door or a window, which is measured by vertical elements.

Beaux-Arts—an eclectic style derived from the blending of classic Greek, Roman, Renaissance, and Baroque influences. It was perpetuated by American architects who studied in Paris at L'École des Beaux Arts. It was popular from the 1890s until the early 1900s.

Bungalow—an early 20th-century residential architectural style that grew from the Arts and Crafts movement of the late 19th century. The style was inspired by a house type found in India in which a central living area is surrounded by verandas and sleeping porches. Characteristic elements include overhanging, bracketed eaves; wide engaged porches; and informal interior floorplans with built-in cabinets, bookshelves, and large fireplaces.

Chamfered—the way a cut is made in wood, usually at a 45-degree angle, as in chamfered support posts on an exterior porch.

Clerestory—a portion of an interior that rises above adjacent rooftops. For example, clerestory windows might be found in watchtowers.

Corbel—a projection from the face of a wall or chimney designed to support structural or decorative elements. For example, see the chimneys on the Currituck Beach Light Keepers House.

Dependencies—outbuildings, wings, or quarters that are subordinate to a main building or house.

Dormer—a window that projects from a roof slope. Types of dormers include: gabled, hipped, shed, or eyelid.

Eave—the projecting edge of a gabled roof.

Elevation—a drawing or design that represents an object or structure as being projected geometrically on a vertical plane parallel to one of its sides.

Engaged porch—a porch attached to the main structure by an extended, uninterrupted roofline.

Fenestration—the arrangement of windows along a facade, an elevation, an interior wall, or within a room.

Gable—a triangular, pitched roof.

Gothic Revival—an architectural design style characterized by steeply pitched roof, cross gables, decorated vergeboards, exterior walls that extend to the gable ends, and one-story porches.

Massing—a type of arrangement of the primary geometric components of a building.

Pier—a rectangular support pillar, often made of wood block, brick, or masonry.

Prairie style—an architectural style attributed to Frank Lloyd Wright that first appeared in Chicago between 1900 to 1920. Characteristic elements include two-story structures with a low-pitched roof, overhanging eaves, and one-story wings, terraces, and porches. Exterior details, such as chimneys, windows, and landscaping, emphasize the horizontal planes inherent in this style.

Rake—the slope or pitch of a roof.

Sidelight—glazing or glass around the periphery of a door frame.

Surround—the border, casing, or area around a window, door, cabinet, fireplace, or sink.

Transom—a window or window configuration above a door.

Vernacular—a non-academic, local expression used in a particular region.

Weatherboards—horizontal boards planed into a wedge, which are used as siding over a timber frame.

Index